Merry Christmas
2019

Love
Aunt Cathy

More! From the Restaurants of PARK CITY

A Mountain Town's **Cookbook**

Enjoy a Taste of **PARK CITY** Restaurants
in Your Own Kitchen

TWO

Lauren Nadler / Park City Publishing / Park City, Utah 2016

Dedication

To my husband, Roger, my boys Cameron and Nick, who
are enjoying their exciting careers in New York City
and to Molly, the cutest and most lovable dog in the world.

Published by Park City Publishing / Lauren Nadler Designs.

Published in the United States by Park City Publishing and Lauren Nadler Designs, Park City, Utah.

Cover and Book Design by Lauren Nadler

ISBN: 978-0-9975910-2-6

Printed in China.

Introduction: Letter from the Publisher

A growing mountain town, Park City has become a "Food Mecca" with award winning chefs and restaurants. As a skier in Park City for many years, I remember the restaurants, bars, pubs, and clubs just as much as the powder and days on the slopes. Skiing has always been the major focus of the town, but has broadened significantly with an amazing range of biking and hiking trails to suit all abilities. Add the fabulous restaurants to this adventure to make for a perfect holiday or lifestyle in any season.

This book is my way of saying thank you to Park City for providing one of the best living experiences in the world. The first Park City Cookbook has been such a success that I thought a second book would provide an opportunity to feature more of our fabulous restaurants and beautiful scenery.

The recipes presented here were contributed by 19 different restaurants and from each chef, in his or her own words. We have strived to make the recipes as consistent, clear, and 'home-cook' friendly as possible and have added, wine and beer pairings, when able. Serving sizes vary, so feel free to ajust for your party size. Adolph insisted that his recipe quantities remained in grams. He said it adds to his authentic Swiss style cuisine, and we agreed.

Having Adolph's in our second cookbook is proof that restaurants have staying power here in Park City. For the newecomers, we invited Chef Laurel Bartmess and the Woodland Biscuit Company to contribute, not only for her amazing biscuits and sandwiches but, also for the "cuteness factor" of the WBC. In our biking family a ride to Woodland is also known as the biscuit ride.

Cameron Nadler is our in-house wine expert. Cameron is a sommelier at a high profile restaurant in Manhattan. Before NYC he worked here in Park City at the St. Regis J&G Grill. Cameron has always had a love for wine and loves touring the vineyards of California, France, and Italy to find some of the best wines the world has to offer. He has always considered Park City his home away from home and loves the opportunity to help bring some of the lesser known wines of the world to your home, whether it's in Park City, or a small village in the South of France. Because of his passion and knowledge of wine, we asked Cameron to help some of the restuarants with their wine pairing and descriptions. Cameron researched and wrote about the wines Adolph had picked for his dishes. For Cuisine Unlimited, Myrtle Rose, Flanagan's, Molly Blooms, and Snake Creek Grill, Cameron studied their wine lists, when available, to come up with his perfect pairings.

So here's my gift to you, more of the true 'taste' of Park City.

—Lauren Nadler

Acknowledgments

A special thank you to Pat Cone Photography for his beautiful food and scenic Park City images. To my tag team of writers and editors, Stephanie Edelman, Corinne Humphrey and Michelle Battaglia, for making sure the recipes translated well for your kitchens. To Phil Archbold, Bob Christie, and Francis Morgan for their scenic photo contributions. A huge thank you to the restaurants and chefs of Park City, who have contributed their recipes and stories, allowing me to create this exciting book. Further thanks to the supportive friends who have helped along the way.

PARK CITY
189
To Sundance & Provo
HEBER
16.5 Miles
from Park City
40
H
MW
113
MIDWAY
3 Miles from Heber
WOODLAND
21 Miles
from Park City
W
35
Francis
32
Kamas
The Jordanelle Reservoir
EMPIRE PASS
EP MONTAGE
SILVER LAKE
VILLAGE
Ontario Canyon
Empire Canyon
DEER VALLEY
ST REGIS
DV
American
Flag
Marsac Ave
Rosie
Hill
MS
MAIN
STREET
S
E
W
N
To
40
Solamere
189
The Aerie
Deer Valley Drive
Park Ave
PARK CITY
BASE AREA
248
To
Woodland
PROSPECTOR
SQUARE
P
Bonanza
Drive
Prospector Ave
Empire
Ave
SILVER STAR
Hospital
KB
KEARNS
BLVD
224
189
CANYONS
VILLAGE
CV
WALDORF ASTORIA
WESTGATE, HYATT
To Promontory
Swanner Preserve
Bear Hollow
UTAH
OLYMPIC PARK
KIMBALL
JUNCTION
KJ
PINEBROOK
80
To Salt Lake City
Silver Creek Junction
Exit 145
Jeremy Ranch

CONTENTS
and Key Code

CV Canyons Village DV Deer Valley EP Empire Pass H Heber KB Kearns Blvd KJ Kimball Junction MW Midway MS Main Street P Prospector

A Appetizer S Soup/Salad E Entrée SD Side Dish D Dessert C Cocktails

MORE!

From the Restaurants of

PARK CITY

ADOLPH'S

SWISS SKI

ADOLPH'S

KB

International flags greet you at the door of this casual fine dining restaurant pleasing patrons in Park City since 1974. With its wood-paneled walls, soft candlelight, vintage ski posters and European décor, Adolph Imboden has created a warm and cozy atmosphere that is reminiscent of an alpine hideaway you might find in a Swiss mountain village. The lively bar scene is the perfect place for après-ski gatherings—share a ski cocktail and traditional fondue or Raclette within view of Park City resort's slopes located just a few blocks away. As Park City grew into an international resort, Adolph's attracted many of the visiting rich and famous including skiers, golfers, cyclists and entertainers from Jack Nicklaus and Arnold Palmer to Dustin Hoffman and Robert Redford to the Swiss and the US ski teams. Now their photos adorn the walls adding to the intimate and inviting setting. A former ski racer himself, Adolph caters to international athletes who crave a taste of home.

Adolph's menu offers a variety of traditional Swiss dishes such as Raclette, Swiss Cheese Fondue, Beef Bourguignon, "Roesti" and Wienerschnitzel. Additional house specialties include Escargot de Bourgogne, Rack of Lamb, Duckling a L'Orange, Chateaubriand, Filet de Boeuf "Oscar," as well as selections of fish, chicken, pasta and seasonal items. Chef Adolph's early love of photography took a backseat to carrying on the family restaurant tradition. "I'm a better chef than photographer," he says. But his photographer's eye is evident in the beauty of the dishes that leave his kitchen—each plate is a work of meticulous attention to color, presentation and of course, taste. Desserts, for those who still have room, are all homemade and especially enticing. Try the Bananas Foster, Cherries Jubilee, Peach Flambé or the ever popular Carrot Cake with Hot Apricot Glaze and Marzipan Carrots, and of course the Swiss chocolate fondue.

In addition to the accolades from repeat customers, Adolph's has won numerous awards over the years, including "Distinguished Alpine Dining" and "Certification of Excellence" from Trip Advisor. All serve to reinforce what Adolph learned from his mother: offer high quality, consistently good, fresh food that will turn customers into friends and keep them coming back again and again.

EXECUTIVE CHEF ADOLPH IMBODEN

As a young man growing up in the Jungfrau region of Switzerland, Adolph learned the restaurant business first-hand in his mother's restaurant kitchen. She taught him "never take shortcuts, use the best ingredients and stay consistent." That early lesson has been the basis of his culinary career. After his apprenticeship in two ot the best hotels in Gstaad, the Palace Hotel and the Victoria Jungfrau Hotel in Interlaken and the prestigious Hotel School in Lucerne, Switzerland, Adolph taught skiing in St. Moritz. While instructing the rich and famous, including the Shah of Iran, during a private lesson Adolph met somone who introduced him to the owner of Deer Valley and was offered a job as Food and Beverage Manager for the Park City Resort. That was in 1971. By 1974 he *(cont'd on page 4)*

Raclette Swiss Style

12 oz raclette cheese, 3 oz per person
8 small white potatoes, boiled
8 pickles, (cornichons preferred)
8 pearl onions, (boiled and peeled)
8 grape tomatoes
parsley
paprika

Raclette cheese is available in most cheese stores. The best Raclette cheese is from Switzerland and France. It can be served as an appetizer or as a meal.

Slice the cheese on an oven proof plate and melt under salamander or broiler until cheese is melted, but not burned or browned, about 4-5 minutes.
Clean and boil white poratoes. Boil and peel onions.

Serve with boiled potatoes, pickles, pearl onions and a few grape tomatoes.
Sprinkle the top of the cheese lightly with paprika and serve immediately while cheese is still melted to perfection.
Garnish with parsley.

Serves 4

(bio, cont'd from page 3) *opened his own place named "Adolph's White House", the golf course restaurant was next and then at his present location on 1500 Kearns Blvd.*

RACLETTE *comes from the word racler which means "scraping off". For this Swiss dish, raclette refers to the scraping off of the melted cheese from the wheel of cheese that is melted over a fire to reach an optimal softness, and then scraped on top of bread.*

Adolph's Original Swiss Cheese Fondue

1-2 garlic cloves
300-400 ml (10-12 oz) of dry white wine (Swiss Pendant)
350 g (12½ oz) Swiss gruyere cheese
350 g (12½ oz) Swiss emmental cheese
10-15 g (1-2 tsp) corn starch
20 ml kirsch (2 oz) (use only Swiss/German made)
freshly ground pepper and nutmeg
600 g (20 oz) of good bread with crust,
  cut into ½ inch pieces
apples cut into thin slices
potatos, cooked and cut into large cubes

Rub the inside of a fondue pot with the garlic. Add the white wine and bring it almost to boiling point. Grate the Swiss gruyere and emmental cheeses into a bowl and then slowly add the cheese to the pot using a wooden spoon, stirring constantly. When the mixture almost reaches a boiling point again, add the corn starch and kirsch. Then add pepper and a little nutmeg.
Transfer the pot to a fondue burner and serve immediately.

Have your desired dipping items separate and ready to serve. Bread cut in ½ inch pieces, apples sliced, potatoes.

Recommend serving with a glass of dry white wine, tea, and at the end, a 2 oz glass of kirsch. Ideally, there should be 4 people at one fondue pot.

Serves 4

"Even today the term fondue is used all too often for various blends of ingredients which do not inevitably produce culinary successes. This recipe, however, is quite authentic, has not been dreamed up, but is rather the legacy of many generations."

—Adolph Imboden

WINE PAIRING *Adolph Imboden recommends:*
ROBERT GILLIARD Fendant Les Murettes (Valais, Switzerland) 2012. Adolph's perfect choice for his fondue. A pale yellow color, this wine bursts on the palate with aromas of pear, citrus, and a hint of yeast. The nose of this wine accentuates the fondue perfectly. When you combine both wine and cheese your mouth should taste bits of pear, apple, and a double-cream brie cheese.

FONDUE *originated and promoted as the Swiss national dish, became popular in the United Stares in the 1930's. Specifically, it is a communal pot of melted cheese kept soft over a chafing stand and heated with a candle or spirit lamp. The meal process with long-stemmed forks dipped into the cheese with various breads or vegetables.*

Veal Adolph's with Rösti

KB | E

VEAL ADOLPH
450 g (16 oz) veal, thinly sliced by hand
300 g (10½ oz) calf's kidney, thinly sliced
80 g (2½ oz) butter
salt and pepper to taste
80 g (2½ oz) shallots, chopped
150 g (6 oz) fresh mushrooms, thinly sliced
100 ml (3½ oz) white wine
100 ml (3½ oz) brown stock
200 ml (7 oz) fresh cream
zest of lemon
parsley, chopped

RÖSTI
50 g (¼ cup) butter
50 g (¼ cup) raw bacon, cut in small pieces
80 g (⅓ cup) onions, chopped
900 g (4 cups) potatoes
roughly grated parsley or chives, chopped
salt and pepper to taste

The original Swiss dish is called Sliced Veal Zurich Style, or "Kalbsgeschnetzeltes." There are many different interpretations of this recipe, but no better compliment has ever been paid to the chefs of Zurich than that of a writer and gourmet who ranked their "Kalbsgeschnetzeltes" among the world's 100 best dishes.

Melt butter in a sauté pan. Season the veal and kidney slices with salt and pepper and sauté quickly. Remove from pan and keep hot.

Chop shallots, slice mushrooms, and season both with salt and pepper. In another sauté pan sweat the seasoned shallots and mushrooms. Deglaze the pan with white wine. Add brown stock to the pan and cook for 2-3 minutes.

Remove the shallots and mushrooms and thicken the stock with "beurre manie." Add the cream, meats and mushrooms to the mixture stirring gently. Re-heat, but do not cook more. Add the lemon zest.

Beurre Manie
Add flour and butter and knead until it is mixed and broken up into particles of butter covered with flour.

Rösti
Melt the butter in a stove top sauté pan. Chop bacon and onions and add to the melted butter to sweat until the onions are translucent.
Grate the potatoes and add to the mixture. Add part of the chopped herbs (parsley or chives). Add salt and pepper.
Spread the mixture over the bottom of the pan and cook until brown. Flip the mixture over and brown the other side.

Plate veal Adolph, top with parsley and serve with "Rösti" sprinkled with the remaining chives and/or parsley.

serves 5

WINE PAIRING *Adolph Imboden recommends:*
CHATEAU D'AUVERNIER Pinot Noir (Neuchâtel, Switzerland) 2013. A Pinot Noir pairs perfectly with a Veal, so why not have a glass of a fantastic Swiss produced Pinot. This ruby red in color pinot is overflowing with red fruits and even a hint of hazelnut will really bring out all the flavors of the veal. With this recipe the red fruits of the wine perfectly combines the mushrooms, basil, and meat elements of the dish. We highly recommend a glass or a bottle from Adolph's cellar.

BEURRE MANIÉ *is a dough made of butter and flour used to thicken soups and sauces. Unlike roux, you do not cook beurre manie. Instead, knead the butter and flour together to create small particles of butter coated with flour. As the butter melts it releases the flour into the sauce or soup without creating lumps.*

Rack of Lamb

KB | E

two 12-14 oz New Zealand
spring rack of lamb
¼ tsp white pepper
⅛ cayenne pepper
¼ tsp paprika

CHERVIL BUTTER
2 oz unsalted butter
1 fresh garlic clove, finely chopped
1 small onion, finely chopped
1 Tbsp parsley, chopped
1 Tbsp chervil, chopped
1 Tbsp lemon juice
1 tsp salt
¼ tsp white pepper
⅛ cayenne pepper
¼ tsp paprika
¼ tsp Aromat Swiss seasoning
(found at most local markets)
and a splash, (or more) bit of brandy

Adolph's house specialty!

Preheat oven to 350 degrees.

Chervil Butter

Mix in a small bowl. Add to softened butter, chopped garlic, onion, parsley, and chervil, add lemon juice, salt, white pepper, cayenne pepper, paprika, Aromat Swiss spice and the splash of brandy.

Rack of Lamb

Spice rub the rack of lamb with salt, white pepper, cayenne pepper, and the paprika.
In oven-proof pan, brown the racks in a frying pan on both sides, then place in the oven at 350 degrees and cook for approximately 15 minutes. Lamb is best when pink between medium rare and medium.

Assembly

Heat up the chervil butter, plate the rack of lamb and top with chervil butter.
At Adolph's this house specialty is served with homemade mashed potatoes and two fresh vegetables du jour.
Mint jelly is always a nice addition to this lamb dish.

Serves 2.

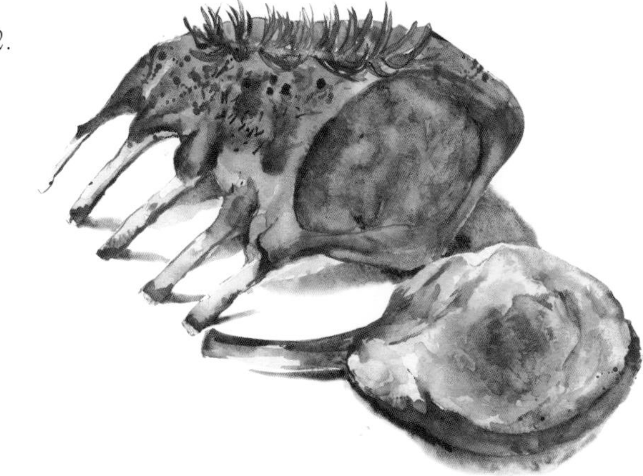

WINE PAIRING *Adolph Imboden recommends:*
CHATEAU D'AUVERNIER Pinot Noir (Neuchâtel, Switzerland) 2013.
A Pinot Noir pairs perfectly with a Veal, so why not have a glass of a fantastic Swiss produced Pinot. This ruby red in color pinot is overflowing with red fruits and even a hint of hazelnut will really bring out all the flavors of the veal. With this recipe the red fruits of the wine perfectly combines the mushrooms, basil, and meat elements of the dish. We highly recommend a glass or a bottle from Adolph's cellar.

AROMAT SEASONING *is a Swiss blend of herbs and spices, found in your local market. Aromat can be used like salt and pepper, for cooking or at your table for an extra added flavor to your dishes.*

Adolph's Carrot Cake

KB | D

5 eggs, separated
300 g (10½ oz) sugar
juice of 1 lemon
zest of 2 lemons
300 g (10½ oz) carrots, finely grated

300 g (10½ oz) almonds, ground
75 g (3 oz) corn flour
pinch cinnamon
pinch ground cloves
10 g (2 oz) baking powder
pinch salt

50 ml (2 oz) kirsch
30 g (1½ oz) apricot jelly for glazing

ICING
fondant icing/marzipan carrots

This carrot cake is now a Swiss classic, its reputation having been extended long ago far beyond the borders of Switzerland. Some maintain that the cake is better two days after baking as the carrots keep it moist.

Preheat oven to 180 degree celsius (350 degrees farenheit).
Separate the eggs. Beat together egg yolks, sugar, lemon zest and lemon juice.
Grate the carrots, ground the almonds and add to the egg/lemon mixture.
Mix in the corn flour, cinnamon, ground cloves and baking powder and mix well. Then add the kirsch.
Beat the egg whites until stiff and carefully fold into the mixture.
Place the mixture in a sponge tin 24 cm (10 inches) in diameter and 5 cm (2 inches) high.
Bake for 1 hour.
When cooked, brush the cake with a hot apricot glaze and thin fondant icing. Decorate with small marzipan carrots.

WINE PAIRING *Adolph Imboden recommends:*
MAD CUVEE Late Harvest Tokaji 2012: If theres one type of wine that is great with dessert, it's a Tokaji. The Mad Cuvee Royal Tokaji is absolutely superb. The nose has a fantastic aroma of quince, pear, and gingerbread spices that will allow for the carrot cake spices to really burst in your mouth. The finish on it will allow for the wine to really sit on your palate while you enjoy every bite of the cake.

Adolph- Thank you for
all you taught me-
Your friend Stein 11/19-99

APEX
AT MONTAGE

APEX AT MONTAGE

EP

Apex, Montage Deer Valley's signature on-mountain restaurant, is a celebration of progressive American cuisine presenting creative takes on classic American dishes, offering guests a relaxed, yet refined, dining experience. The menu is an inspired revival of iconic dishes focused on fresh local ingredients prepared with care and presented in remarkable style.

The setting, tucked within Empire Pass overlooking the aspen groves and trails of the resort, complements the cuisine, creating an elevated dining experience that is unique within the mountain destination. Serving breakfast, lunch and dinner, Apex offers a warm ambiance to enjoy any meal of the day. Guests have the option throughout the year to take their dining experience outdoors on the slope-side Apex Terrace and soak in the rays of the sun or the glow of the fire pits at night time.

Throughout the ski season, skiers and guests alike can enjoy the breakfast and skier's buffets featuring live action stations and an array of sweet and savory dishes. For wine connoisseurs, a team of certified sommeliers are available to help pair and explore varietals from the extensive wine list featuring labels from around the world.

The culinary team shares a passion for serving authentic farm-to-table food and therefore creates menus that change with the seasons. Working with local purveyors, the ingredients used are found in Utah - Gold Creek Farms' artisanal cheese, Strong Vertical Gardens' vegetables and Heber Valley's Creamery cheeses, to name a few. Providing high quality products that are sourced locally, chefs present some of the most inspired fresh and unique flavors within the state of Utah.

EXECUTIVE CHEF SHAWN ARMSTRONG

With a culinary career spanning two decades and several continents, Shawn Armstrong brings a world of experience to Montage Deer Valley. With almost five years at Montage, Armstrong oversees signature Apex, all of the culinary creation and execution and also the expansive Banquets department.

Armstrong became recognized for his award-winning cuisine at high-profile venues in South and Southeast Asia, including the Oyster & Wine Bar Restaurant in Hong Kong, the Maldives Islands' Taj Coral Reef Resort and Singapore's The Cliff Seafood Restaurant, earning a Three-Chef-Hat rating. At-Sunrice, the premiere culinary academy in Singapore, Armstrong was named Global Chef of the Year. Prior to joining Montage, Armstrong held the role of Executive Chef of the Mandarin Oriental Las Vegas.

Golden Beet and Tomato Gazpacho with Shrimp, Avocado & Heirloom Tomato Salsa

EP | A

3 golden beets, roasted, peeled, diced
2 yellow tomatoes
½ shallot, sliced
1 garlic clove, crushed
2 Tbsp sherry wine vinegar
1 tsp sugar
½ cup extra virgin olive oil
2 cups vegetable stock or water, cold

SHRIMP AND AVOCADO SALSA
8 shrimp, peeled, poached, diced
1 avocado, peeled, seeded, diced
2 oz cherry tomatoes, halved
1 Tbsp extra virgin olive
salt to taste

Preheat oven to 350 degrees.

Roasted Beets

Cut off tops of beets. Clean and peel with vegetable peeler. Dice, then lightly coat beets with olive oil and roast for 30 minutes, turning several times while roasting.

Poached Shrimp

In a large pot, or poaching dish if you have one, add a few inches of water, add a pinch of salt and bring to a boil. Reduce heat to medium, then add the shrimp. Simmer for 5 minutes until the shrimp are pink and curled. Remove from heat, cool and dice.

Gazpacho

Combine roasted beets, tomatoes, shallot, garlic, vinegar, and sugar and blend in blender until smooth. Slowly drizzle in ½ cup extra virgin olive oil until emulsified and adjust consistency with vegetable stock. Adjust seasoning to taste.

Shrimp and Avocado Salsa

Combine diced shrimp, avocados and tomato halves with 1 Tbsp olive oil and season with salt.

Assembly

Divide soup into 4 bowls and garnish with the shrimp and avocado salsa

---

CHEF CHRISTIAN OJEDA *Chef de Cuisine of Apex, joined Apex Montage Deer Valley in 2014 with an impressive culinary background highlighted by his experience in many highly acclaimed luxury hotels and restaurants. Before joining Montage, Ojeda served as Executive Chef at Calistoga Ranch and as the Chef de Cuisine at Encantado in Santa Fe. Chef Ojeda has also worked at Fleur de Lys and Joel Robuchon in Las Vegas, as well as Santa Fe's award-winning Geronimo, where he played a vital role in the restaurant as Executive Sous Chef. Ojeda graduated from the Art Institute of Colorado with a BA in Culinary Management. In his position as Chef de Cuisine, Chef Ojeda oversees the Apex culinary team, utilizing his distinctive blend of classic European, progressive American and Southwestern culinary expertise.*

WINE PAIRING *Dave Wallace recommends: MORGADÍO Albariño, (Rias Baixas, Spain).*

Black Tea Crusted Ahi Tuna with Pickled Mango, Avocado & Cucumber Escabèche

GREY GHOST CRUSTED AHI TUNA
two 3 oz sashimi grade Hawaiian Ahi Tuna (block cut)
2 Tbsp olive oil
salt and pepper to taste

ATTICUS GREY GHOST BLACK TEA CRUST
3 Tbsp ground Atticus Grey Ghost Black Tea
½ tsp ground mustard seeds
¼ tsp ground ginger
¼ tsp ground coriander seeds
¼ tsp ground black pepper

PICKLED MANGO
¾ cup seasoned rice vinegar
1 cup granulated sugar
2 Tbsp sea salt (substitute, kosher salt)
½ tsp fresh sliced ginger
1 ½ cups sliced green mango

AVOCADO PEA PUREE
1 ripe avocado
½ cup frozen peas (defrosted)
zest and juice of half a lemon
pinch of garlic powder, salt and white pepper

CUCUMBER ESCABÈCHE
¼ cup finely diced English cucumber, seeds removed
2 Tbsp finely diced Roma Tomatoes, seeds removed
¼ tsp minced pickled ginger
zest and juice of half a lemon
½ tsp chopped chives
1 Tbsp extra virgin olive oil

Atticus Grey Ghost Black Tea Crust
Place tea, mustard seeds, ginger, coriander and black pepper into a spice grinder and grind until mixture resembles a fine powder.

Pickled Mango
In a small sauce pot add vinegar, sugar, sea salt and ginger, and bring the mixture to a boil. Once the sugar and salt have dissolved, pour over mangos and refrigerate for 24 hours.

Avocado Pea Puree
Combine avocado, peas, lemon zest and juice, garlic powder and salt and pepper in a small food processor and blend until smooth. Alternately, use a fork to mash together. Set aside. Serve well chilled.

Cucumber Escabèche
Finely dice cucumber and tomatoes, avoiding seeds as much as possible. Then add all ingredients into a small mixing bowl and season with salt and pepper. Allow to chill for 1 hour.

Assembly
Season tuna with salt and lightly coat with tea mixture.
In a skillet, heat 2 Tbsp of olive oil over medium-high heat. Gently place the seasoned tuna in the skillet and cook 30 seconds to 1 minute per side for rare. Once the tuna is seared, place it in the refrigerator for 10 minutes, to prevent further cooking of the fish. Slice the tuna into thin slices, sashimi style. Shingle the tuna slices onto a plate and dress lightly with the cucumber escabèche. Arrange the plate with dots of pickled mango and avocado puree.

CHEF OJEDA TIPS *If you do not have a grinder, a coffee grinder or blender will work to grind the spices, or you may purchase all spices in ground form. The black tea mixture can be stored for up to 1 month in an airtight container. Alternatively, for the Pickled Mango, you may puree the mangos or simply slice and serve to save time on cooling.*

WINE PAIRING *Dave Wallace recommends: KUNG FU GIRL Riesling, (Washington State).*

Pan Roasted Foie Gras with St. Germaine Fruit Cocktail, Vanilla Crème Fraiche & French Toast

four 3-4 oz foie gras, escalope
4 oz seasonal fruit, diced
2 Tbsp St. Germaine liquor
1 Tbsp white balsamic
2 Tbsp sugar

½ cup milk
2 eggs, whole
2 tsp cinnamon, ground
½ vanilla bean
2 brioche toast, thick slice, cut in half

CRÉME FRAICHE
½ cup crème fraiche
(store bought or homemade)
1 cup whipping cream
2 Tbsp buttermilk

St Germaine Fruit cocktail

Combine fruit, St. Germaine liquor, white balsamic, and 1 Tbsp sugar. Let marinade for 15 minutes or up to 2 hours.

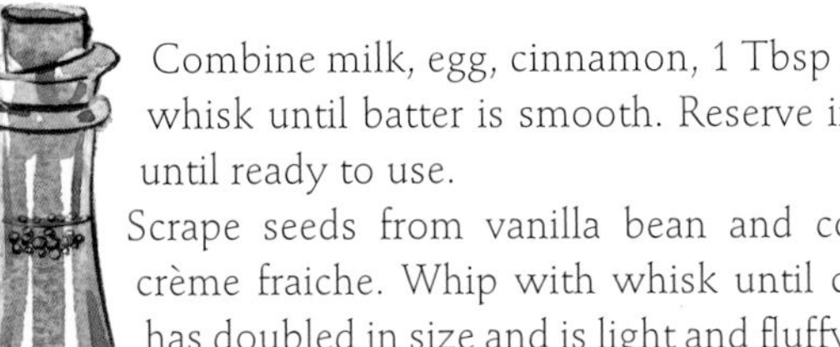

Combine milk, egg, cinnamon, 1 Tbsp of sugar, and whisk until batter is smooth. Reserve in refrigerator until ready to use.

Scrape seeds from vanilla bean and combine with crème fraiche. Whip with whisk until crème fraiche has doubled in size and is light and fluffy. Refrigerate.

Heat non-stick pan over medium heat, and coat pan with film of blended oil. Dip brioche toast into milk/egg batter, and cook on each side 1 to 2 minutes. Keep warm while proceeding to cook the foie gras.

Créme Fraiche

You can use store bought créme fraiche or, if you prefer, you can make your own homemade créme fraiche by combining whipping cream and buttermilk in a glass container. Stir well, cover and let stand at room temperature for 8 to 24 hours, or until very thick. Refrigerate for up to 10 days.

Foie Gras

Heat sauté pan over high heat. Cook foie gras escallopes about 1 to 2 minutes per side until just cooked through. Season after cooking with a pinch of sea salt.

Assembly

Spoon crème fraiche on plate. Top with French toast, foie gras, and garnish with fruit cocktail. Chef Armstrong recommends topping the dish with edible flowers and toasted pistachios.

BEVERAGE MANAGER OF MONTAGE DEER VALLEY, Dave Wallace has paired our recipes with a pick from our extensive wine list. Dave started with the company during the opening of Laguna Beach in 2003. His enthusiasm for the industry began years ago during his Laguna Beach days, when he developed a love for guest interaction, the camaraderie of the team and the creative freedom that it provides - from creating cocktails and wine lists, to entire beverage programs, along with training and mentoring others on their journeys.

Shortly after opening Montage Laguna Beach, Wallace further developed his expertise with a Court of Master Sommeliers and Advanced Bartending and Master Mixologist certification. He then went on to open each Montage property, including the opening of Palmetto Bluff in September of 2016.

Working with the industry's most talented chefs is also a major highlight of Dave's passions by having the opportunity to match culinary creativity with his expertise in wines and unique beverages.

WINE PAIRING Dave Wallace recommends:
ROYAL TOKAJI WINE CO., Red Label, 5 Puttonyos, Hungary.

Guanciale Wrapped Pork Tenderloin with Farro Risotto, Brussels Sprouts & Fruit Mostarda

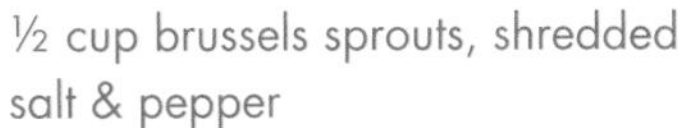

FARRO & BRUSSELS SPROUTS RISOTTO
- 1 cup farro
- 4 cups water
- 6 cups chicken stock
- 4 Tbsp olive oil
- 1 shallot
- ⅓ cup dry white wine
- ⅓ cup heavy cream
- ½ cup brussels sprouts, shredded
- salt & pepper

GUANCIALE WRAPPED PORK TENDERLOIN
- 20 thin slices Guanciale or bacon
- 2 pork tenderloin, cleaned of silver skin
- ½ cup canola oil
- salt & pepper to taste

STONE FRUIT MOSTARDA
- 1 tsp oil
- 1 shallot, minced
- 2 cups diced stone fruit (apricot, peaches, etc)
- 1 Tbsp mustard seeds
- ¼ cup white wine vinegar
- ⅛ cup light brown sugar
- ½ Tbsp Dijon mustard

Heat oven to 450 degrees.

Farro & Brussels Sprouts Risotto

Combine farro with 4 cups water and soak for 30 minutes. Drain well and set aside.

Heat the chicken stock in a sauce pan and keep warm.

Heat oil in Dutch oven or heavy based stock pot. Sweat shallots until translucent. Add drained farro and stir constantly until toasted, about 3 minutes. Add wine and stir constantly until evaporated.

Add warm chicken stock, ½ cup at a time, until well absorbed and farro is tender.

Add Brussels sprouts and cream, and cook, stirring constantly, for about 2 minutes. Season to taste with salt and pepper.

Stone Fruit Mostarda

Heat 1 tsp of oil over medium head and sauté shallots until translucent. Add stone fruits and mustard seeds for about 1 minute. Deglaze with vinegar and reduce by half, adding sugar and Dijon mustard. Simmer on low for 5 minutes. Cool and set aside.

Guanciale Wrapped Pork Tenderloin

On a flat surface, lay 10 guanciale or bacon slices out vertically with edges slightly overlapping, creating a "sheet" of pork goodness. Season pork tenderloin with salt and pepper and lay on top of "bacon sheet" horizontally. Bring ends of "bacon" over tenderloin and continue to roll, completely covering tenderloin with edges, overlapping by at least an inch. Repeat with second tenderloin.

Place wrapped pork tenderloin on roasting rack over a sheet pan and bake until internal temperature of 145 degrees is reached, about 10 minutes. Remove from oven and cover loosely with foil for 5 minutes. Once cooled, remove foil, trim ends and cut tenderloins into 4 equal portions. Serve with risotto and mostarda.

(Serves 4)

CHEF'S TIP Chef Ojeda suggests making the worthwhile trip to Salt Lake's Tony Caputo's Italian Market and Deli to find the guanciale. Caputo's house-made guanciale will make this dish a standout as it has a wonderful earthy quality that is only found in this product.

WINE PAIRING Dave Wallace recommends: PENNER ASH Pinot Noir, (Willamette Valley, Oregon).

Baba Black and Tan Ice Cream

19 oz whole milk
4 oz heavy cream
1 vanilla bean, scraped and seeded
6 oz sugar

5 oz brown sugar
5 egg yolks, fresh
salt, pinch

3½ oz Black Baba Lager, Uinta Brewing Co.
ice cream machine

Place milk, cream and vanilla bean in a pot and bring to simmer. In a separate bowl, whisk together sugars, egg yolks and salt. Slowly stir in small amounts of the hot dairy mixure into yolk mixture until all has been incorporated.
Place back on medium-low heat and, using wooden spoon, stir and cook gently until liquid reaches 82 degrees celcius (180 degrees farenheight) or until mixture is thick enough to coat back of the spoon. Chill immediately.
Once liquid is cold, stir in the beer and refrigerate overnight.

Yields 2 pints of ice cream.

Process in an ice cream machine according to your manufacture's instructions and freeze for at least 3 hours.
Enjoy with caramel sauce and crushed toffee pieces.

EXECUTIVE PASTRY CHEF STEPHEN JONES *Joined the culinary team in 2015. Executive Pastry Chef Stephen Jones brings an extensive background to Montage.*

A native of New York, Jones received both his Pastry Arts and Business and Hotel Management degrees at the Culinary Institute of America, where he had the opportunity to be instructed under Certified Master Pastry Chef Joseph McKenna. Upon graduation, Jones joined the Bellagio Hotel and Spa in Las Vegas where he received extensive training under Top Pastry Chefs Chris Hamner and Claude Escamilla. Soon after, he opened the JPM Patisserie directly under MOF (Meilleur Ouvrier de France) Pastry Chef Jean-Philippe Maury, and by age 22, landed his first Executive Pastry Chef position at the Four Seasons Palo Alto.

After continuing his career in luxury resort settings, and prior to joining Montage, Jones achieved one of his professional goals and opened his own co-founding patisserie, Vers Restaurant and Patisserie, in Chatham, Massachusetts.

Chef Jones' passion is to find new trends and techniques that can help expand his knowledge and imagination in Pastry Arts, and has traveled around the globe to seek inspiration. His approach is that of using modern innovated techniques along with classic disciplines. He has had the privilege to work under six World Pastry Championship gold medalists, and most recently trained under world-renowned chocolatier Melissa Coppel.

WINE PAIRING *Dave Wallace recommends:*
COSSART GORDON Madeira, 5 yr. Bual, Portugal

Blue Boar Inn
Blue Boar Inn
& RESTAURANT

THE BLUE BOAR INN

The Blue Boar Inn, nestled in the peaceful foothills of Midway, Utah, is an old-style European Inn named after the tavern from Howard Pyle's classic children's novel, *The Merry Adventures of Robin Hood*. Winner of AAA's Four Diamond Awards for both the Inn and the restaurant every year since 2010, and winner of numerous Utah "Best of State" awards, the Blue Boar Inn has attracted a loyal local and international clientele. It also boasts the highest Zagat rating of 26 and Wine Spectator's "Award of Excellence" for their extensive wine selection.

Executive Chef Eric May creates a seasonal array of signature items that reflect American and European techniques and cooking methods, often incorporating fresh herbs from the Inn's gardens. "Many dishes on the menu have Scandinavian and German influences," says Chef May, "and I like to add my own twist." Menus change seasonally, but the escargot, fondue and classic schnitzel are perennial favorites. The Inn is open every day for breakfast, lunch and dinner, and a five-course brunch is served on Sunday. Come on Wednesday nights to enjoy the Chef's Prix Fixe Menu.

The moment guests enter the lobby, with its river rock columns, antler chandeliers and hand carved staircases, they are embraced by an aura of romance and warmth. Start your Blue Boar experience in the walnut-paneled Truffle Hollow Pub, where you can enjoy appetizers or a full dinner with a view of Snake Creek Canyon and surrounded by European antiques, including a 16th Century hand-carved bar and an authentic wooden crossbow. Each of the Inn's 12 guest rooms and suites, named after famous literary figures like Geoffrey Chaucer, Robert Frost and Jane Austen, are accented with fireplaces, European pillow-top beds and jetted tubs. The "Hinterhof" Patio, German for "patio behind," is a perfect summer dinner or event venue surrounded by magnificent gardens and majestic views of the Wasatch Mountains.

Located adjacent to three breathtaking golf courses, Wasatch State Park, Sundance Resort, and some of the best skiing and fly-fishing in the country, the Inn's charming ambiance allows guests to escape their everyday surroundings for an evening, an overnight or for a week-long stay.

EXECUTIVE CHEF ERIC MAY

Chef Eric May earned an Aeronautical Degree from the University of North Dakota. Realizing a flight instructor's salary wouldn't pay the bills, he ditched that flight path to follow his true passion of cooking.

After graduating from ICE Culinary School in New York, Eric began his career at Water's Edge in Long Island City. Later, as sous chef at Man Ray in Manhattan, he created meals for Bono, Johnny Depp and other celebrities. He advanced to Executive Sous Chef at L'Escale in Greenwich, Connecticut's Delamar Hotel before migrating to Utah in 2004. Eric became Chef de Cuisine at Homestead Resort's Simon's restaurant, earning multiple AAA Four Diamond Awards. As Executive Chef/GM of the Blue Boar Inn, he has appeared on CBS, ABC and Fox 13, and continues to win accolades including the ICE Alumni Hall of Achievement Award.

Coriander Cured Gravlax

MW | A

2 lbs center cut salmon fillet, skin on

CORIANDER CURE
4 Tbsp coriander seeds
2 Tbsp caraway seeds
1 Tbsp white peppercorn
1½ lbs kosher salt
1 lb brown sugar
2 oz fresh dill

DILL MUSTARD SAUCE
2 Tbsp heavy cream
4 Tbsp Dijon mustard
1 Tbsp lemon juice
1 Tbsp red wine vinegar
2 Tbsp chopped fresh dill
5 Tbsp olive oil

GARNISHES
2 hard-boiled eggs
1 diced shallot
½ cup capers
pumpernickel toast

Cure Salmon

Toast the coriander, caraway seeds and white peppercorn, then coarsely chop in a spice grinder (you could also use a mortar/pestle). Transfer to a mixing bowl. Add the salt and brown sugar and combine. Put a third of the rub and a third of the fresh dill on the bottom of a glass baking dish. Lay the salmon on top, skin side down. Rub the remaining cure mix on top of the salmon. Cover with plastic wrap, then place a plate on top. Place heavy cans on top of plate. Refrigerate 24-36 hours.

Rinse the cure mix off of the salmon with cold water. Pat dry with paper towels, then allow to dry fully in the refrigerator, uncovered, for 1-3 hours.

Dill Mustard Sauce

In a medium bowl, whip the heavy cream until it forms soft peaks. Add the Dijon mustard, lemon juice, vinegar and dill. Whisk until fully incorporated. Slowly drizzle in the olive oil while whisking so mixture is fully emulsified. Refrigerate for 1 hour before using.

Garnish

Hard boil the eggs. When they are cooled, separate the yolk (crumble) and the egg white (small dice). Thinly dice the shallot. Refrigerate until ready to use.

Assembly

Slice the salmon very thinly (almost transparent), and place on serving platter. Cut toasted pumpernickel bread into triangles. Make "rows" of egg whites, yolks, capers and shallots alongside salmon. Add a dollop of mustard sauce.

Serves 10 appetizer-size portions.

WINE PAIRING *MOREAU, Chablis 1er Cru Vaillon, (Chablis, Burgundy, France) 2011.*
Always a great pairing, Chablis and Gravlax. Christian Moreau has been a staple of Chablis for years. This wine starts off with a burst of green apple followed by a fantastic nose of mineral and citrus aromas. A perfectly focused and clean wine. It is well balanced with citrus, apple, and minera notes as well. Medium plus finish.

Wild Mushroom Manicotti

MANICOTTI FILLING
5 Tbsp extra virgin olive oil
2½ lbs mixed mushrooms (1 lb shitake, ½ lb oyster, ½ lb button, ½ lb shimenji)
2 Tbsp chopped shallots
2 tsp chopped garlic
salt and pepper
2 Tbsp chopped parsley
2 Tbsp chopped chives
½ tsp chopped thyme
½ tsp chopped rosemary
8 oz Boursin cheese
½ cup grated Gruyere cheese
1 egg
1 egg yolk

CREPES
1½ cups water
1 cup all-purpose flour
3 eggs
½ Tbsp kohser salt
½ tsp sugar
2 Tbsp gruyere cheese, finely grated
1 tsp chopped chives
2 tsp chopped parsley
non-stick cooking spray

MORNAY SAUCE
2 oz butter
2½ Tbsp all-purpose flour
2 cups milk
½ tsp sea salt
pinch cayenne pepper
pinch nutmeg
8 oz grated Gruyere cheese
8 oz shredded Parmesan cheese
pinch white pepper

Manicotti Filling

Sauté the mushrooms in oil, then add shallots and garlic. When lightly browned, add salt and pepper to taste. When cool, place half of mushroom mixture in food processor. Pulse until it has a coarse texture. Transfer to a mixing bowl, and fold in the herbs, cheeses and eggs. Store in the refrigerator until ready to assemble.

Crepes

In a blender, mix the water, flour, eggs, salt and sugar. Pour into a large bowl. Stir in the cheese, chives and parsley. Refrigerate for one hour. Spray and heat a 6-inch non-stick pan. Pour about 1 oz of the batter and swirl the pan to make a thin and even crepe. When the edges start to curl, flip it and cook for 10-15 seconds. Repeat with the rest of the batter.

Mornay Sauce

In a medium heavy saucepan, melt the butter and add flour to make a roux. Add milk and bring to a simmer over medium heat. Add sea salt, cayenne pepper, nutmeg, Gruyere cheese, Parmesan cheese, and pepper and cook until thick, stirring constantly.

Assembly

Preheat oven to 350 degrees. Put about 2 Tbsp of the filling on each crepe and roll up. Place on baking sheet and bake for 10 minutes. Place on serving dish. Pour the Mornay sauce over crepes. Top with the rest of the sautéed mushrooms.

Serves 6

WINE PAIRING *ADELSHEIM Pinot Noir (Willamette Valley, Oregon) 2011. I had this for the first time at the Sundance Resort and I'm glad Blue Boar has it as well. This Oregon pinot has a broad display of red aromas such as candied cherry, pomegranate and raspberry. If you search into the flavors you will find a light touch of brown spices; nutmeg, cinnamon, all-spice. It finishes off with integrated, silky, and polished tannins.*

Roasted Trout

four 6-ounce trout (butterfly and debone)

CITRUS VINAIGRETTE
¼ cup orange juice
¼ cup lemon juice
½ Tbsp Dijon mustard
1 tsp chopped shallot
1 clove garlic, chopped
salt and pepper
1½ cups olive oil

YUKON GOLD POTATO ROUNDS
3 potatoes, sliced into
½ inch rounds
3 cups extra virgin olive oil
1 tsp sea salt
1 sprig rosemary
4 sprigs thyme
10 black peppercorns
2 bay leaves
2 cloves garlic

VEGETABLES
1 cup Brussels sprouts leaves
½ cup sliced red onion
½ cup asparagus tips
½ cup grape tomato halves
½ tsp garlic, minced
1 cup lardons (or bacon)
salt and pepper

Citrus Vinaigrette

In a blender, blend all ingredients, except oil, until smooth. Slowly add olive oil in a steady stream while blender is running. Set aside until ready to use.

Yukon Gold Potato Rounds

Cut the potatoes into ½-inch rounds. In a large pot, submerge the potato rounds with the rest of the ingredients and bring to a simmer. Cook until fork tender, about 15 minutes.

Lardons

In a sauté pan, brown the lardons (or bacon) until crispy.

Assembly

Preheat oven to 350 degrees.

Heat 1 Tbsp of oil in a 12-inch non-stick pan. When it starts to smoke, place the trout skin side down. When trout turns opaque, place it in the oven on an oven-safe platter for 2-4 minutes.

Sauté the vegetables until wilted. Add the lardons and the potatoes. Heat evenly, then scatter on top of the fish. Drizzle with vinaigrette and serve.

Serves 4

WINE PAIRING *CUPCAKE Chardonnay (Central Coast, California) 2013. A medium to full bodied wine is what you want with a Trout dish. Cupcake Chardonnay is perfect. The Chardonnay is barrel aged which allows for a wine rich and exploding with flavors of white peach, honeycrisp apple, apricot and lemon meringue. As the glass opens up you taste fresh hazelnut, almonds, and vanilla begins to form along with some subtle spice and toasted oak flavors. A balanced acidity, bright fruit flavors and a creamy mouth feel fills the palate, creating a lovely finish.*

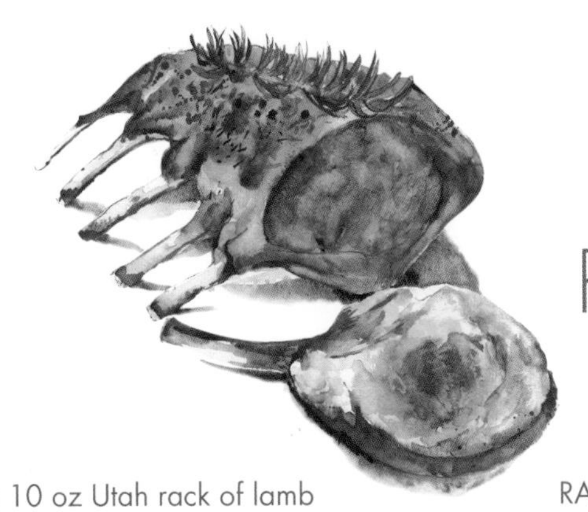

Rack of Lamb

six 10 oz Utah rack of lamb

LAMB SAUCE
2 lbs lamb bones and scraps
can of olive oil spray
1 onion, chopped
1 carrot, chopped
1 clove garlic, chopped
2 cups red wine
4 cups beef broth

RATATOUILLE
1 yellow onion, diced
2 zucchini, diced
2 yellow squash, diced
1 eggplant, diced
1 clove garlic, chopped
salt and pepper
8 oz. Boursin cheese
2 zucchini, sliced lengthwise

HERBES DE PROVENCE
2 Tbsp lavender
2 Tbsp dried basil
2 Tbsp dried thyme
2 Tbsp dried marjoram
2 Tbsp dried parsley
2 Tbsp dried savory
4 bay leaves
salt and pepper

Preheat oven to 375 degrees.

Lamb Sauce

Spray lamb bones and vegetables with olive oil spray and brown in the oven. Transfer to a pot, add the wine and broth and bring to a boil. Reduce heat and simmer until reduced to 2 cups. Strain and set aside.

Ratatouille

In a skillet, sweat the onion until translucent. Add chopped zucchini, squash, eggplant and garlic and saute until soft, but still firm. Add salt and pepper to taste. Let vegetable mixture cool completely. Once cooled, mix with Boursin cheese.

In the meantime bring 4 cups of salted water to a boil and blanch the sliced zucchini until pliable. Shock the blanched zucchini in ice water to keep the color vibrant. Pat dry. Put 2-3 Tbsp of ratatouille mixture on the zucchini slices and roll up carefully.

Rack of Lamb

Preheat oven to 450 degrees.
Grind all the Herbes de Provence in a spice grinder.
Pat the lamb dry and rub with Herbes de Provence and salt and pepper. Add oil to a skillet and brown lamb on all sides. (You can probably fit 2 racks per batch). Transfer lamb to a roasting pan and roast at 450 degrees for 10-15 minutes until internal temperature reaches about 120 degrees. (Pull lamb out of oven about 5 degrees below desired doneness and allow for carry-over cooking.)

Cut the rack into 2 chops per plate. Warm the sauce and place about a ¼ cup on each plate. Place chops on the sauce. Arrange ratatouille rolls and serve.

Serves 6

WINE PAIRING *CASTELLO DI BOSSI, Chianti Classico, (Tuscany, Italy), '09. I always prefer a Chianti with lamb. It always pairs well because of the ripe berries that are always brought out perfectly. With this fantastic recipe a Chianti would be perfect. This wine is a deep, ruby-red in color. It offers a blend of aromas such as ripe cherries and red plums. These flavors are overlayed with subtle notes of toasted vanilla beans and wildflowers. On the palate, the wine displays a well-structured balance of bright acidity and a savory finish.*

Chocolate Crusted Cheesecake

OREO CRUST
26 pieces Oreo cookies, finely crushed
½ Tbsp sugar
¼ cup melted butter

FILLING
2 lbs cream cheese, softened
1 ⅓ cups sugar
4 Tbsp cocoa powder
4 eggs, room temperature
10 oz bittersweet chocolate, melted and cooled

Preheat oven to 350 degrees.

Make the Crust

Grease a 9-inch springform pan. Mix Oreo crumbs with sugar and melted butter. Press onto the bottom of the pan and bake for 5-7 minutes. Let cool.

Make the Filling

Using an electric mixer with a paddle attachment, mix cream cheese and sugar on high speed. Mix in cocoa powder. At low speed, add 1 egg at a time. Add melted chocolate until well blended. Pour batter into cooled crust and even out the top.

Lower oven temperature to 275 degrees. Place the cake in a roasting pan and add enough hot water to the roasting pan to come about a quarter of the way up the sides of the cake pan. Bake for 90 minutes until the center of the cake is set.

Serve with mixed berries and whipped cream.

Serves 8

WINE PAIRING *Graham's Fine Tawny 20 Yr (Porto, Spain) N/V. One of my favorite after-dinner drinks is a Tawny Port. Cheesecake and Port go hand in hand. This port has a delicious combination of dried figs, caramel, dried raisins and coffee beans. Its full-bodied, sweet and delicious which shows a fantastic amount of length and beauty. It will pair perfectly with your chocolate crusted-cheesecake.*

Cuisine Unlimited

CUISINE UNLIMITED

CUISINE UNLIMITED

P

Cuisine Unlimited was founded by Maxine Turner in 1985 as a small deli and catering operation. The business grew quickly and Maxine's husband, Marvin, left his corporate accounting job to help with operations of the flourishing company, which eventually included construction of the current catering kitchen and offices to meet the demand for the 2002 Winter Olympics.
Cuisine Unlimited has been a part of several different national and international projects. We have been involved in varying degrees with five different Olympic Games and supported catering operations for the 2008 Republican National Convention in Minneapolis and the PGA Tour in Chicago.

In addition to countless weddings and social occasions, Cuisine Unlimited contributes to a variety of local business, non-profit and community events. We have catered the Salt Lake Dining Awards, provided concessions for the Red Butte Garden Summer Concert Series for many years and managed all food operations for the Eccles Theater in downtown Salt Lake City.

Though originating in Salt Lake City, Cuisine Unlimited has developed a strong business presence in Park City and is an active member of various associations in the area. From conferences to weddings, we cater a multitude of events at various Park City venues. You can find our food services at Newpark Resort, All Seasons Resort, and Hugo Coffee Roasters. Each year, Cuisine Unlimited takes part in Savor the Summit alongside restaurants of Park City's Historic Main Street. We are also one of two preferred caterers for the Sundance Film Festival, providing food and beverage services for more than 75 official festival and sponsor events each year, including the Closing Awards Celebration and After Party.

With unlimited options, we can develop custom menus and décor to meet any event or theme. We specialize in all types of cuisine, from traditional Jewish fare to modern Cuban fusion. Now managed by Maxine's sons, Aaron and Jeff, Cuisine Unlimited has expanded to a true, full-service event provider. With more than 100 employees today, Cuisine Unlimited is proud to serve a variety of clients in the entire Utah community, the United States, and around the world.

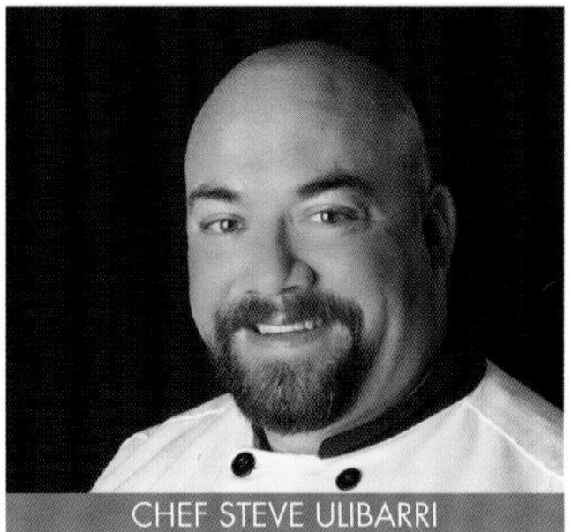
CHEF STEVE ULIBARRI

Hailing from Los Angeles, California, Steve Ulibarri has been the celebrated executive chef of Cuisine Unlimited since 1997. Head of the professional catering kitchens for Cuisine Unlimited Catering & Special Events, Steve is unwavering in his commitment to excellence in service, cuisine, and creativity, proving to be a master of many cooking styles. He is valued for his innovation as he brings new culinary techniques and ideas for presentation to the kitchen.

Steve has trained and mentored many students and takes pride in educating his staff to the nuances of fine foods. He conducts classes for the Park City Culinary Institute and appears on many local TV programs providing food demonstrations. He has proven leadership skills and works regularly on positive teambuilding and motivational development activities.

PG34 PG35 PG36 PG37 PG38

CUISINE UNLIMITED

Forest Mushrooms in Romesco Sauce

ROMESCO SAUCE
2 medium red bell peppers
3 pasilla peppers (can be omitted, or substituted with other chile peppers)
6 plum tomatoes
¼ cup olive oil
½ large onion, chopped
1 garlic clove
¼ cup slivered almonds
2 Tbsp plus 1 tsp sherry vinegar
1 tsp sweet paprika

BASIL OIL
4 cups basil
1 cup canola oil

MUSHROOMS
4-5 per serving assortment of mushrooms (reccommended enoki, trumpet, and oyster)
grapeseed oil
kosher salt

Roast the bell pepper and pasilla peppers until consistently charred, then transfer to a bowl. Cover for 10 minutes.
Score tops of tomatoes with an "x" and drop in boiling water. When the skin starts to fold back, transfer the tomatoes to an ice bath.
After about five minutes, take tomatoes from the ice water and peel the skin off. Cut in half and remove seeds.
Once peppers have cooled, peel the skin and cut in half to remove seeds.
Put the olive oil in a pot on medium heat and add onion, tomatoes, and peppers and let simmer for 5 minutes.
Add the remaining ingredients and cook for 5 minutes, stirring constantly.
Transfer to a blender and blend until smooth. Salt and pepper to taste.

Mushrooms
Sear mushrooms in a hot pan with oil until caramelized. Season with salt.

Basil Oil
Puree the basil with oil in a blender.
In a cooking pot, bring to a simmer over medium heat.
Immediately remove from heat.
Pour into a bowl lined with cheesecloth.
Fold edges of cheesecloth together and tie to form a pouch.
Hang pouch at least 2 hours over a container to catch basil oil.
Separate romesco sauce between serving dishes and top with mushrooms. Garnish with basil oil.

Yields 4-6 servings

WINE PAIRING SEA SMOKE, Ten, Pinot Noir, Central Coast, California, 2012. For those of you wine enthusiasts out there Sea Smoke is as not as well known as Screaming Eagle or Opus One, but it is truly one of the best Pinot Noirs this side of the Atlantic. Sea Smoke Ten is from ten different clones from ten different parcels they own. They say that it is the pinnacle of Pinot Noirs, and who are we to dispute that claim. More of a burgundy stylization, the experience begins with a nose of lavender and dark cherry. Then comes a plethora of spices, blueberries, and finished with a bit of a dusty slate flavor to give that nice minerality. The finish is long and velvety.

CUISINE UNLIMITED

Carrot and Ginger Soup with Fresh Mascarpone

1 lb carrots, chopped
1 medium yellow onion, diced
2 tsp garlic, minced
3 Tbsp olive oil
½ tsp granulated sugar
½ tsp salt
¼ tsp pepper
2 tsp minced ginger
2½ cup chicken stock
2½ cup water
4 Tbsp mascarpone cheese

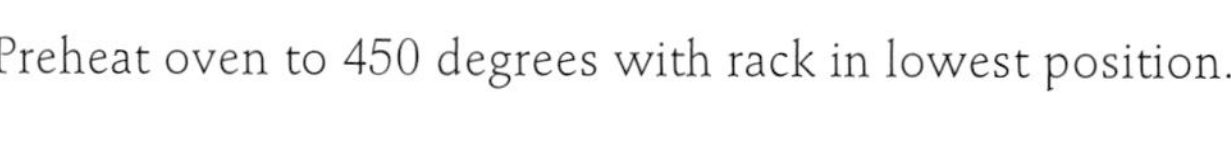

Preheat oven to 450 degrees with rack in lowest position.

Chop carrots and toss with onion, garlic, olive oil, sugar, salt, and pepper.
Spread in a 4-sided sheet pan and roast in the oven, stirring occasionally, until browned and tender, 25 to 30 minutes.
Blend half of the roasted vegetables in a blender with ginger and chicken stock until very smooth. Transfer to a medium saucepan. Repeat with remaining vegetables and water.
Thin to desired consistency with extra water and simmer 2 minutes. Season with salt and pepper.

Assembly

Separate into four small bowls. Just before serving, top each bowl with a tablespoon of mascarpone cheese.

Tips

Garnish with a pinch of turmeric for added color and flavor.
Mascarpone cheese can be substituted with sour cream.
Chicken stock may be substituted with vegetable stock for a vegetarian alternative.

Yields 4 servings

WINE PAIRING *BROOKS, Ara Reisling, Willamette Valley, Oregon 2009. This Willamette Valley Reisling would cut through the ginger extremely well. The bouquet of fresh fruit, full of citrus notes; nectarine, tangerine and oranges would give your taste buds a great complement to the ginger snap flavor. The wine also has beautiful aromas of orange blossom, honeysuckle and white flowers. The herbal notes include sage, chervil and tarragon that complements the soup's flavor.*

CUISINE UNLIMITED

Frisee & Quinoa Salad with Lemon Vinaigrette

2 cups vegetable stock
1 cup red quinoa
1 fennel bulb, cored and quartered
2 Tbsp grapeseed oil
1 large carrot, peeled

1 head frisee, chopped to approximately 2 inch pieces
¼ cup pine nuts
½ cup shaved Parmesan

LEMON VINAIGRETTE
1 cup lemon juice
1 shallot
1 tsp Dijon mustard
2 Tbsp maple syrup
3 cups canola oil

Bring vegetable stock to a boil over high heat. Add quinoa, and simmer covered over low heat for 20 minutes. Transfer to a sheet pan to cool.

Core the fennel bulb and cut into fourths. In a medium skillet, heat oil over medium heat. Add fennel and toss until caramelized. Salt to taste.

Cut carrot into thirds and slice as thin as possible. Place carrots into a strainer, then into a bath of ice water until slices have started to curl. Remove from water and allow to dry.

Lemon Vinaigrette

Toss frisee with lemon vinaigrette.

In a blender, combine lemon juice, shallot, Dijon mustard, and maple syrup. Slowly add canola oil until mixed evenly.

Assembly

Divide quinoa onto four plates and top with frisee, carrots, and fennel. Garnish with pine nuts and shaved Parmesan.

Yields 4 servings

WINE PAIRING *KIM CRAWFORD Savignon Blanc, Marlborough, New Zealand, 2014. This wine, from "down-unda," A go-to Sauvignon Blanc, is perfect to pair with this salad. The citrus and tropical flavors brimming from this wine allows for your taste buds to cut through the acidity of the lemon vinaigrette in a classic way. While there are some citrus flavors in this wine the tropical sweetness allows for the perfect balance between the two. This will allow for you to pair the salad and wine with every bite.*

Pan-Seared Barramundi with Tomato Cucumber Relish

BARRAMUNDI
four 6 oz boneless, skin-on barramundi filets
3 Tbsp vegetable oil

TOMATO CUCUMBER RELISH
1 lb roma tomatoes, diced
1 English cucumber, peeled and diced (may substitute a regular cucumber)
½ bunch flat leaf parsley (approximately 1oz)
¼ cup capers
3 Tbsp olive oil
3 Tbsp red wine vinegar
1 lemon

GREEN RICE
1 cup parsley, roughly chopped, lightly packed
½ cup cilantro, roughly chopped lightly packed
2 large poblano chiles, seeded and roughly chopped
2 Tbsp chopped green onion
1 garlic clove, peeled and roughly chopped
3 Tbsp canola or grapeseed oil
1½ cup long grain white rice
2¼ cups vegetable stock
salt to taste

Tomato Cucumber Relish

Dice the tomatoes and cucumbers. Chop parsley. Mix all ingredients in a bowl and season with salt to taste. Refrigerate for at least an hour to allow flavors to combine.

Green Rice

In a blender or food processor, purée parsley, cilantro, chiles, onion, garlic, and 1/2 cup of stock until smooth.
Heat the oil in a thick-bottomed pot over high heat. Add the rice and stir to coat all of the grains with oil. Spread out in an even layer. Let the rice lightly brown. When most of the rice has lightly browned, add the purée mixture. Stir to combine thoroughly, and cook for 1-2 minutes.

Add the remaining vegetable stock to the pot. Bring to a boil, then reduce the heat to a low simmer and cover the pot. Let cook on a very low simmer for 15 minutes.

Let cool for 2 minutes, then divide and place on four serving dishes.

Barramundi

Heat oil in a heavy skillet or cast-iron pan, over medium heat. Once oil is smoking, add barramundi filets skin side down. Season with salt and pepper to taste.
Cook 3-5 minutes, depending on thickness, then flip over and cook other side for 3-5 minutes.
Remove from pan, and set atop rice. Top with relish and serve.

Yields 4 Servings

WINE PAIRING *MARCEL LAPIERRE MORGON, Burgundy, France, 2014. This beaujolais is fantastic with fish. The 100% Gamay varietal is a lighter, more tart/acidic version of a Pinot Noir. A lot of people don't always like reds with fish, however this one will give your move a fantastic flavor of light fruits such as strawberries and cherry. It will also give a nice hint of sweet tannins and a medium to long finish that will stay with you as you enjoy the relish.*

Chocolate Pot de Creme

6 dark chocolate squares
1/3 cup cocoa, unsweetened

3 egg yolks
1/3 cup granulated sugar

1 cup heavy cream
1 cup milk

Melt the dark chocolate and cocoa together in a double boiler. You can also use a large stainless steel bowl over a stockpot of boiling water.

In a large mixing bowl, whisk the egg yolks and sugar together. Set aside.

In a large saucepan, heat the cream and milk together until it is scalding or almost to a boil. Remove from heat.

Whisk the cream and milk mixture very slowly into the eggs and sugar. You want to slowly warm the eggs so they don't cook too quickly and curdle. Add all of the cream and milk mixture to the bowl to incorporate with egg mixture.

Pour combined mixture back into the large saucepan and bring to a simmer, stirring constantly with a wooden spoon for about 5 minutes, or until the mixture coats the back of the spoon.

Slowly whisk the custard mixture into the melted chocolate.

Pour into 4 individual ramekins and cover immediately with plastic wrap to avoid a film from forming on top of the custard.

Let cool at room temperature for 10 minutes, then refrigerate for at least an hour. This recipe may be made days ahead.

Tips

Once set, you can top the pot de crème with caramel or fruit coulis to add another flavor note to the chocolate custard. Top with fresh berries just before serving for a fresh and tasty addition.

Garnish with edible flowers to add color and enhance the presentation of your dessert.

Yields 4 servings

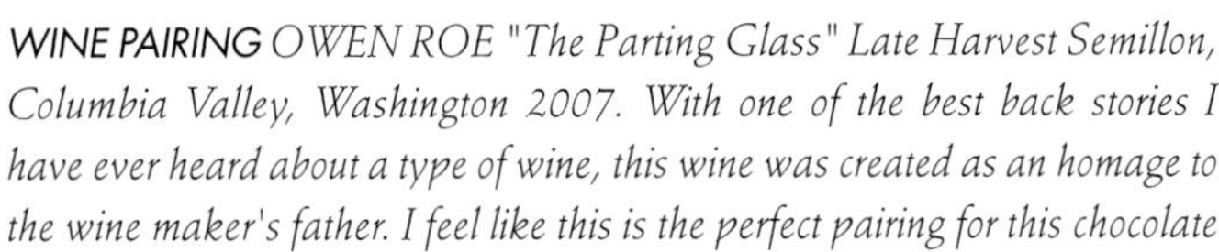

WINE PAIRING *OWEN ROE "The Parting Glass" Late Harvest Semillon, Columbia Valley, Washington 2007. With one of the best back stories I have ever heard about a type of wine, this wine was created as an homage to the wine maker's father. I feel like this is the perfect pairing for this chocolate dessert. An American producer from the Columbia Valley in Washington state created this fruity bouquet of ripe golden delicious apple, pear, and kumquat. This will give you a fruity burst in your mouth as you bite into the chocolate pot de creme.*

FREE TROLLEY
HISTORIC
FREE
MAIN STREET
PARK CITY TRANSIT
41078

Drafts
SPORTS BAR & GRILL

DRAFTS

CV

Conveniently located in the Canyons Village area of Park City Ski Resort, Drafts is a gastropub offering an eclectic wine list and a fully stocked bar where expert mixologists concoct classic cocktails and specialty drinks like adult milkshakes and Mojito or Moscow Mule popsicles. Try the "Un-Kosher Bloody Mary" made with High West vodka and smoked maple bacon foam. Beer aficionados will also appreciate Drafts' selection of over 50 draft and bottled beers from around the world. The comfortable tin-ceilinged interior houses a lively, kid-friendly gathering place where patrons can view their favorite national and international sporting events on high definition large screen televisions; outside, the heated deck is a perfect venue to enjoy après-ski with views of the Canyons Village resort plaza and the Wasatch Mountains.

Drafts strives to deliver superior food and service, and that effort has not gone unnoticed. In an annual contest run by the Park Record newspaper, Drafts was recognized by local Parkites as having the best wings and the best french fries two years in a row. Additionally, Drafts earned TripAdvisor's "Award of Excellence" and was awarded "Best American Pub" and "Best Gourmet Burger" by Utah's "Best of State" competition every year from 2013 through 2016.

Thanks to new Chef Jess Everson and a talented kitchen staff, Drafts' menu continues to evolve. Customers clamor for their famous Shrimp Tacos, a tasty entrée of three warm corn/flour hybrid tortillas stuffed with grilled cilantro lime shrimp, cabbage, house-made pico de gallo and a drizzle of chipotle ranch dressing. The Coconut Shrimp Salad and crispy Tachos, tater tots topped with melted cheese sauce, bacon, sour cream, chives, diced tomatoes and vegetarian or buffalo beef chili, are also popular items. Be sure to save room for their unique Dessert Pizza--crusty goodness topped with cream cheese, brownie bites, fresh raspberries, chocolate syrup and a dusting of cinnamon sugar. Look for new chicken waffles, sous vide items and a breakfast sandwich to be added to the 2016/2017 winter menu. Drafts is open daily for breakfast, lunch and dinner during the winter ski season, and serves lunch and dinner only in summer.

CHEF JESS EVERSON

Salt Lake City native Jess Everson initially studied architecture at University of Utah. "It was too restrictive," he says. "I liked working with my hands, and I loved food—I was always experimenting with cooking at home."

At age 19, Everson turned his passion into a career path, entering the Cordon Bleu Culinary School in Las Vegas. While in school, he worked at various establishments where he learned about inventory, ordering, and recipe development. "I learned so much about managing a kitchen in those early years." After graduating, Everson became Head Chef at Salt Lake City's Cliff House Gastro Pub before being lured to run Drafts' kitchen. At Drafts, he combines his classical French culinary training with a desire to make food 'relatable' and fresh, creating inventive gourmet pub fare.

PG44 PG45 PG46 PG47

Shrimp Tacos

CV | A

twelve 6″ flour or corn tortillas
1 lime, cut into 8 wedges
1 lb 16/20 peeled and deveined shrimp
1 lime, zest and juice
2 Tbsp vegetable oil

PICO DE GALLO
2 tomatoes
¼ red onion, diced
1 jalapeno pepper, diced
¼ cup cilantro, chopped
juice from1 fresh lime
salt to taste

CABBAGE MIX
¼ head red cabbage
¼ head green cabbage
2 carrots

CHIPOTLE RANCH DRESSING
16 oz ranch dressing
1½ Tbsp chipotle pepper powder
2 tsp cumin

Split all shrimp down the middle and place in a mixing bowl. Add oil, lime zest and lime juice. Mix well, cover, and let marinate for 30 minutes.

Pico de Gallo

Dice tomato, onion, and jalapeno. Chop cilantro.
Place tomato, onion, jalapeno and cilantro in a mixing bowl with a pinch of salt. Mix together thoroughly with rubber spatula. Add another pinch of salt if desired.

Cabbage Mix

Shred red and green cabbage and carrots into mixing bowl and toss with tongs to mix.

Chipotle Ranch Dressing

Place ranch dressing, chipotle pepper powder and cumin into mixing bowl and whisk together to combine thoroughly.

Sauté or grill marinated shrimp for about 60 seconds or until cooked through. Shrimp will turn pink and curl slightly.

Assembly

Warm tortillas in oven, then place ¼ cup cabbage mix on each tortilla and top each with 3 shrimp.
Top shrimp with 1 oz pico de gallo, then drizzle with chipotle ranch dressing.
Garnish with lime wedges.

Serves 4.

BEER PAIRING WASATCH BREWERY, Provo Girl, German pilsner. A Bavarian pilsner style beer, the type you find in the Munich area of Germany. With a crisp, clean golden colored brew, Magnum hops, Provo Girl is then lagered, (cold storage) for 30 days for superb drinkability.

Coconut Shrimp Salad

CABBAGE MIX
¼ head red cabbage
¼ head green cabbage
2 carrots

SWEET CHILI LIME VINAIGRETTE
½ qt Mae Ploy Thai sweet chili sauce
½ cup sriracha sauce
¼ cup lime juice
¼ cup rice wine vinegar
¾ cup vegetable oil
¼ cup granulated sugar

COCONUT SHRIMP
12 medium shrimp,
  peeled and deveined, tail-on
3 eggs
1 cup flour
1 cup panko crumbs
1 cup dried sweetened coconut flakes

8 oz chopped romaine lettuce
½ oz daikon radish sprouts
1 oz crispy wonton strips
½ avocado
¼ English cucumber

Preheat frying oil to 325 degrees.

Cabbage Mix

Shred red and green cabbages and carrots into mixing bowl and toss with tongs to mix.

Sweet Chili Lime Vinaigrette

Place Mae Ploy Thai sweet chili sauce, sriracha sauce, lime juice, rice wine vinegar, vegetable oil and granulated sugar into a blender, and blend thoroughly until smooth.

Coconut Shrimp

Use three separate containers for breading: place flour in one container; in second container, place the three eggs and whisk until yolks and whites are thoroughly mixed; in third container, mix panko crumbs and coconut flakes together.
Butterfly shrimp. Dip each one into the flour first, shaking off any excess.
Next, dip into egg, making sure entire shrimp gets a good coating of egg wash. Shake off excess.
Lay in panko/coconut mixture and press lightly to make sure mixture sticks to shrimp, covering both sides.
Gently lay in preheated deep fry oil for about 60-90 seconds or until golden brown. Remove and let rest on paper towel to drain excess oil.

Assembly

Place 4 oz chopped romaine on two plates.
In a mixing bowl, place 2 oz cabbage mix and ¼ cup sweet chili lime vinaigrette and mix together (it will look like too much dressing, but when placed on the rest of the salad it is just right)
Place cabbage slaw on top of romaine. Fan 3 large slices of cucumber on side of salad. Place ¼ oz daikon radish sprouts on salad. Slice an avocado, fan it out, and place on side of salad.
Place deep fried coconut shrimp on side of salad. Top with ½ oz crispy wonton strips.

Serves 2

BEER PAIRING *SQUATTERS BREWERY, Live and Let Live, Krystalweizen Filtered Wheat Beer.*
Live & Let Live celebrates a great German tradition in summer beers. Malted wheat, barley and noble hops coexist in harmony to produce a refreshing crystal clear wheat ale - free of judgment.
4% alcohol by volume..

Ghost Burger

CV | E

6 pretzel burger buns (or bun of choice)
6 8oz 80/20 certified Angus beef patties
12 slices smoked gouda cheese
12 slices bacon, cooked
3 oz baby arugula
12 slices tomato
6 slices red onion

GHOST PEPPER BBQ SAUCE
6 Tbsp Franks RedHot® sauce
6 Tbsp water
1½ Tbsp ghost pepper powder
(2 Tbsp cayenne pepper if ghost powder not available)
10 oz favorite BBQ sauce
(spicy base recommended)

Preheat grill.

Season burger patties with salt and pepper, and grill to desired temperature. Top with cheese to melt.

Toast buns. On bottom half place arugula, two slices tomato, and one slice onion.

Place burger with melted cheese on top of prepared bottom bun. Add 2 slices of bacon, one ounce of Ghost Pepper BBQ sauce and crown with toasted top bun.
Serve with French fries.

Ghost Pepper BBQ Sauce

Combine Franks RedHot® sauce, water, ghost pepper powder and your favorite BBQ sauce in bowl. Whisk to mix thoroughly.

BEER PAIRING *TWO ROWS, Dangereaux Farmhouse Ale. With a hazy golden straw color and a big, fluffy head this ale is full of citrus, pine and grass. Some mild hay and Belgian phenols come near the end. Starting with a juicier hop flavor, orange grapefruit and some pith flavors forward. Moderately sweet, grainy malt follows with some clove and coriander spiciness. The finish is moderately dry.*

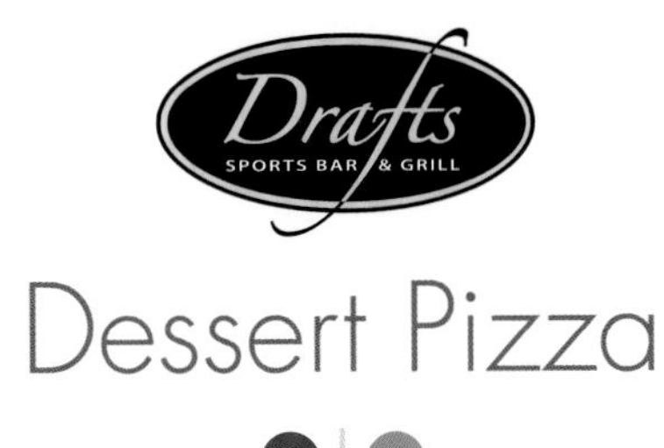

Dessert Pizza

CV | D

DESSERT PIZZA
6 oz pizza dough (either homemade or store bought)
1 tsp cinnamon/sugar mix
3 Tbsp Hershey's chocolate syrup
½ cup brownie (cut into small ½"x ½" cubes)
¼ cup fresh raspberries
vegetable oil spray

CREAM CHEESE FROSTING
4 oz cream cheese
¼ cup powdered sugar
3 fl oz half and half

Preheat oven to 425 degrees

Cream Cheese Frosting

Place room temperature cream cheese in a mixing bowl with half and half and powdered sugar.
Whisk until well combined and it reaches a fluid consistency, adding more half and half if necessary.

Pizza

If using homemade pizza dough, run a dough docker over stretched dough and partially bake on a pizza stone; if using store bought pizza crust, skip to the next step.

Place dough in oven on pizza stone until very lightly browned, or about 80 percent cooked.
Remove from oven. Spray lightly with vegetable oil spray and sprinkle with cinnamon/sugar mix.
Drizzle chocolate syrup over crust and place brownie cubes randomly around the pizza crust.

Bake for another 2 minutes or until chocolate syrup starts to bubble and brownies are heated through.
Remove from oven and let rest for 60 seconds.

Assembly

Cut into quarters. Drizzle with cream cheese frosting and top with fresh raspberries.

(Serves 2)

WHISKEY PAIRING *HIGH WEST DISTILLERY Mid Wnter Night Dram in a snifter. Like Macallan 42 yr, each distillery has their creme de la creme. I personally find that the Mid Winter Night's Dram is that to High West. The rye gives off a beautiful nose of vanilla, caramel, and cinnamon. They age the whiskey in port barrels which also allow for the flavors of plum and dried fruits to really come out. The french oak part of the barrels also allow for a slight accent of spice with a long and fruity finish.*

DOUGH DOCKER *a food utensil used to pierce bread dough. A spiked rolling pin or hand held rotary tiller can also be used. This prevents over-rising or blistering of dough while cooking.*

EDGE
STEAKHOUSE

EDGE STEAKHOUSE

Edge Steakhouse's slopeside setting at the base of Park City Resort's Canyons Village welcomes guests with a stylish elegant interior and chic metropolitan vibe. Edge has a separate exterior entrance, emphasizing the fact that this is a neighborhood destination and not just another hotel restaurant. The low-ceilinged dining room and sleek finishes like the onyx marble bar, dark wood and velvet upholstery give it a more formal feel and make it an ideal spot for intimate romantic dinners, important business meetings or celebratory occasions. The subtle stone accents and warm wood floors are a nod to its mountainside locale.

Edge Steakhouse delivers a cutting-edge culinary experience that takes the traditional American-style steakhouse to a new level. The unique menu blends traditional steakhouse favorites with an array of specialty appetizers, creative entrees and innovative side dishes. The foundation of the menu is the selection of entrees, including top-quality USDA Certified Prime Aged Beef, Wagyu Beef and wild-caught fresh fish and seafood that's flown in daily. Their domestic Wagyu Beef comes from Snake River Farms, which started with a small herd of Wagyu cattle from the Kobe region of Japan. The Wagyu bulls were crossbred with premium American Black Angus and raised with strict standards to produce American Kobe (Wagyu) beef of the highest quality aged for a minimum of 28 days. Edge's USDA prime beef comes exclusively from Niman Ranch.

Edge boasts a full bar with specialty drinks and a great selection of domestic, international and local beers, as well as one of the largest and most comprehensive wine lists in Park City. Since its inception in December of 2012, Edge has won many accolades. With a AAA 4 diamond rating, Edge was also recently named one of USA Today's Top Restaurants in Park City, as well as one of Forbes Magazine's "Top 12 Steakhouses" in the nation. Edge Steakhouse earned the Utah Best of State "Best Steakhouse" award four years in a row and is a two-time "Best of State" statue winner. In addition to being Forbes recommended, Edge has received the Wine Spectator "Award of Excellence," the Trip Advisor "Certificate of Excellence," as well as numerous Open Table awards including "Most Notable Wine List," "Best Steaks" and "Most Romantic Restaurant."

EDGES WINE CELLAR

Edge Steakhouse's wine cellar features over 1100 bottles of wine from some of the best wine producing regions in the world. The glass enclosed backlit wine cave houses a broad selection of wines and champagnes by the glass, half bottle and bottles, including a collection of French Bordeaux 2008 Chateau Margaux, 2005 Chateau Pavie and 2004 La Mission Haut Brion. Wines from Italy, Spain, South America, South Africa, Australia and New Zealand are also on the list. Complete your dining experience with a glass of Sauternes or Graham's Porto Vintage 77.

Edge Steakhouse has garnered numerous awards including Wine Spectator's "Award of Excellence," awarded to restaurants whose wine lists offer interesting selections that are appropriate to their cuisine and appeal to a wide range of wine lovers.

Tableside Wagyu Tartare

TARTARE
4 oz Wagyu beef, diced
1 egg yolk
1 Tbsp Dijon mustard
2 tsp Worcestershire sauce
1 tsp lemon juice
olive oil as needed
1 Tbsp diced capers
1 Tbsp diced cornichons
2 Tbsp brunoise cut red onion
1 Tbsp fine herbs
1 lemon, sliced and grilled
7 crostini toast from French baguette
pepper to taste
1 sliced baguette or crostini

FINE HERBS
1 cup parsley, finely chopped
1 cup chervil, finely chopped
1 cup tarragon, finely chopped
1 cup chives, finely sliced

Tartare

Mix egg yolk and Dijon together until well combined. Add Worcestershire sauce and lemon juice. Slowly add olive oil, stirring constantly until mixture has doubled in volume. Add fine herbs, diced Wagyu beef, capers, cornichons, red onion.

Fine Herbs

In a small bowl combine parsley, chervil, tarragon, chives, and set aside.

Assembly

Form Wagyu beef and herb mixture into a Quenelle or egg shape, and place onto a chilled plate. Add grilled lemon, and angle sliced toasted crostini or baguette to platter and serve.

Serves 4

FINE HERBS *A classic combination of herbs used in French cuisine-usually a fragrant mix of parsley, chives, tarragon and chevril. Sold pre-packaged in most grocery stores.*

Twice Baked Potato

1 large 16-19 oz Idaho baked potato
2 oz grapeseed oil
6 oz truffle salt

6 oz heavy cream
4 oz gruyere cheese
4 oz white cheddar cheese

2 oz diced bacon or lardons
4 oz parmesan cheese
1 Tbsp of sliced chives

Preheat oven to 350 degrees.

Clean potato thoroughly with cold water. Pat potato dry and lather with grape seed oil. Rub generously with truffle salt.
Place potato in 350 degree oven and bake for 45 minutes or until done.
Remove potato from oven and allow to cool for 15 minutes.
Slice potato in half lengthwise, remove potato pulp with spoon, and place in a small mixing bowl. Keep potato skin intact for refilling.

In a small saucepan, warm heavy cream, gruyere and cheddar cheeses over medium-low heat, whisking together until melted and smooth.
Add heavy cream and cheese mixture to potato pulp in mixing bowl. Mix to make desired mashed potato consistency.
Spoon mashed potato mixture back into the potato skin and bake in 350 degree oven for 10 minutes.

With two minutes left, place the lardons or bacon onto the same pan the potatoes are baking on and cook another 2 minutes until crisp. Remove twice-baked potato from oven and garnish with parmesan cheese, chives, and lardons.

serves 2

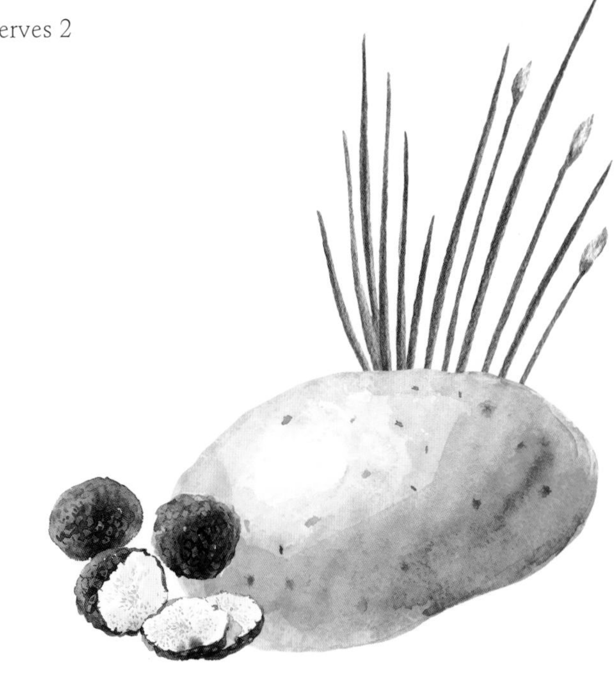

LARDONS OF BACON *can be purchased in the store or you can make by cutting salt cured bacon into small cubes. Salt cure is preferable to smoked bacon.*

Half Chicken Under a Brick

1 whole chicken
2 Tbsp olive oil
8 oz chicken broth
1 cippolini onion, peeled and sliced
2 oz mushrooms, sliced
1 Tbsp butter
4 jumbo asparagus spears
olive oil as needed
salt and pepper to taste
6 oz garlic mashed potatoes

ROSEMARY MARINADE
1oz Rosemary
2oz Garlic
2oz Shallot
6oz Olive Oil
Salt and Pepper to taste

Preheat oven to 350 degrees.

Rosmary Marinade

Mix together rosemary, garlic, shallot, salt, pepper, olive oil.

Chicken

Start at the center of the chicken and gently slice the breast meat away from the breast plate. Glide your knife towards the back of the thigh and carefully remove the thigh from the lower back of the chicken. Now remove the two bone chicken wing from the top of the breast leaving the drum intact.

Mix together rosemary marinade and chicken into sealable bag. Seal and marinate in refrigerator for 24 hours.

Heat a cast iron pan on the stove over medium-high heat for 5-6 minutes. While pan is heating, take an actual brick and wrap it in heavy duty aluminum foil.
When cast iron pan is hot, add 2 Tbsp of olive oil and coat the pan by moving the pan in a circular motion. Remove the chicken from the resealable bag and place the chicken in the pan skin side down. After 4 minutes, put the foil-covered brick on the top of the chicken breast and bake in a 350 degree oven for 15 minutes. After the 15 minutes remove chicken from oven, lift the brick from the back of the chicken, and turn the chicken over to reveal a crispy skin.
Deglaze the pan with the chicken broth and begin to reduce. While reducing, add the mushrooms and cippolini onion. Reduce by half, turn off the stove add the butter.
Slowly swirl the pan and let the butter incorporate with the chicken broth reduction.

Season asparagus with olive oil, salt and pepper and also season to taste on the grill season. Cook until tender.

Assembly

Put half of the garlic mashed potatoes onto the center of each plate. Remove roast chicken from the pan and place on top of the mashed potatoes. Spoon Cippolini onion and mushroom glaze over chicken. Top with roasted asparagus.

Serves 2

WINE PAIRING *ORIN SWIFT PAPILLON Bordeaux Blend (Napa Valley, California), 2013. This Cabernet based left bank style Bordeaux blend will pair beautifully with the chicken dish without overpowering the natural essence of the protein. The notes of rosemary, ripe black cherry and charred meats will do wonders to complement this dish. Enjoy a glass of this garnet colored beauty with an amazing chicken feast.*

Lobster and Black Truffle Risotto

16 oz lobster stock,
(can be purchased in stores)
4 Tbsp grapeseed oil
8 oz Arborio rice
1 onion, brunoise cut

1 carrot, brunoise cut
1 celery stalk, brunoise cut
4 oz white wine
4 oz lobster tail
4 oz heavy cream

2 Tbsp butter
2 oz parmesan cheese
2 oz sliced black truffle
2 Tbsp chives, chopped

Place lobster stock in small sauce pot next and bring to a simmer. "Brunoise cut" the carrots, celery and onion by first julienne slicing, then dice into small cubes about an inch in size. Set the vegetables aside in separate bowls.

In a large sauté pan, warm the grapeseed oil over low heat. Add the Arborio rice and gently toast the rice. Add onion to pan and sauté for 3 minutes. Add carrots and celery, and sauté for an additional 6 minutes, stirring constantly.

Add white wine and stir to combine. When the rice has absorbed the white wine, add 2 ounces of the heated lobster stock and stir. Slowly add the remainder of the lobster stock, stirring constantly. When all the liquid has been absorbed, add the lobster tail, heavy cream, butter and parmesan cheese.

Assembly

Once all the ingredients are cooked, and cheese and cream are melted and blended, place risotto into a bowl or onto a plate. Garnish with sliced black truffle and chives.

WINE PAIRING *PIO CESARE Barolo (Piedmont, Italy), 2010. This classically structured Barolo is, of course, 100% Nebbiolo thus, lending its balanced fruit and mild tannins to the pairing with this fragrant lobster truffle risotto. This red pairs spectacularly with the seafood dish while never overpowering the pallet.*

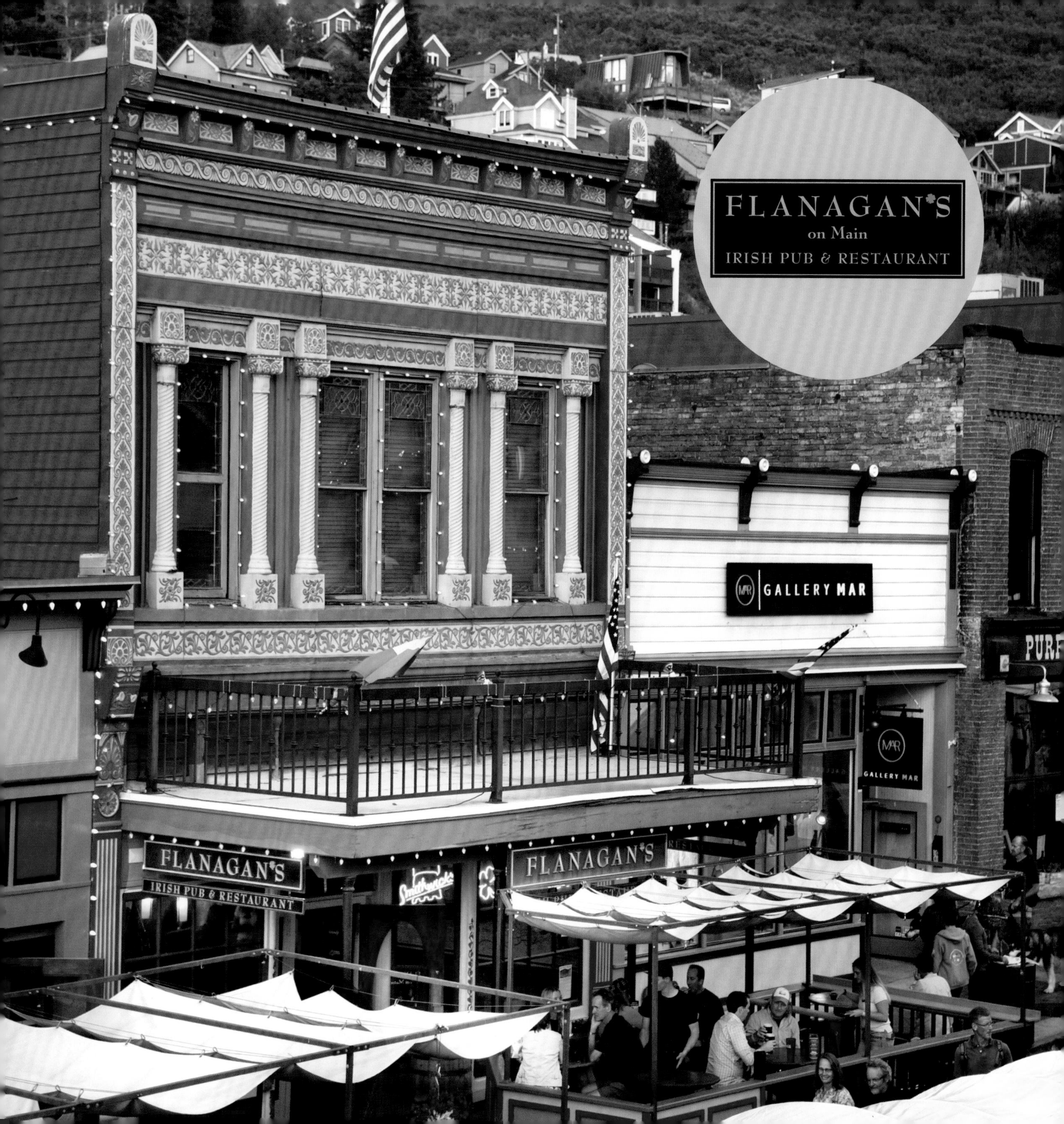
FLANAGAN'S
on Main
IRISH PUB & RESTAURANT
GALLERY MAR
FLANAGAN'S
IRISH PUB & RESTAURANT
FLANAGAN'S
Smithwick's
GALLERY MAR

ESTD 1759
GUINNESS®
BREWED IN DUBLIN

FLANAGAN'S ON MAIN

With deep roots in Park City and the historical district, the building which houses Flanagan's on Main has been a true part of the American West. Constructed at the end of the 1800's, the space served the growing community first as retail space in the early 1900's, followed by a candy company with a soda counter, a juke box and a back room dance floor during the 1930's. Later it housed a series of popular restaurants.

At the turn of the last century in the early 1900's, Father Flanagan of Boys Town fame was traveling across the USA with his troupe of orphaned boy entertainers to raise funds for his dream of a boys' home to be located in Nebraska. Led by one of the rescued orphan boys, Charles (Charlie) Kenworthy, the troupe visited Park City and held fundraising performances in the pavilion directly across the street from 438 Main. The generous citizens made Park City a key stop on their fundraising circuit. Boys Town became a success. Today's owner of Flanagan's on Main is none other than John Kenworthy, Charles' grandson, who is continuing his family tradition of being a key part of his beloved Park City community.

Family friendly, with a full liquor license, this Old Town dining staple is an informal pub with 'good grub' and live music. Relax in the upfront alcove watching the Main Street scene, or cozy up to the bar with a bite and a pint of one of their 12 draft beers, or select from 20 bottled brands. The ultimate man cave downstairs with its 11 television screens is perfect for watching your favorite game. On Friday – Sunday nights, you'll find an intimate music venue for artists that have included members of Bon Jovi, John Popper, and Matisyahu, as well as numerous local acts.

Highlighting menu offerings, start by trying the Dubliner Hot Wings, the Ruben Rolls or the Ahi Tuna Sliders. Authentic Fish & Chips, the Irish Stew, which has been slow cooked in Guinness Stout, and Whisky Chicken Boxty are three of the most popular menu items. A recent award winner of the prestigious "Perfect Pint Award" for the way Flanagan's pour their Guinness with its creamy head, a stop at Flanagan's is a must to enjoy a bit of Park City history as well as great brews, blues and stews.

FATHER FLANAGAN

After earning his degree from Ohio University in Culinary Arts & Hotel Restaurant Management, Chef Greg Walsh perfected his extensive culinary skills across the US, beginning on Hilton Head Island, Georgia, for the Lawry's Group of seasoned salt fame. For the next 23 years, he worked with several of the group's restaurants including the Old Fort Pub and on a sightseeing, guided riverboat dining cruise–voyaging on the historical Savannah River near Jekyll Island, South Carolina. He then went on to Roche Harbor, Washington, with Park City's Stern family group. Greg's considerable talents have brought him back to Park City's Flanagan's on Main, where he ensures the pub's warm and inviting atmosphere is maintained, and ensuring that the menu is as enticing as it is authentic and affordable.

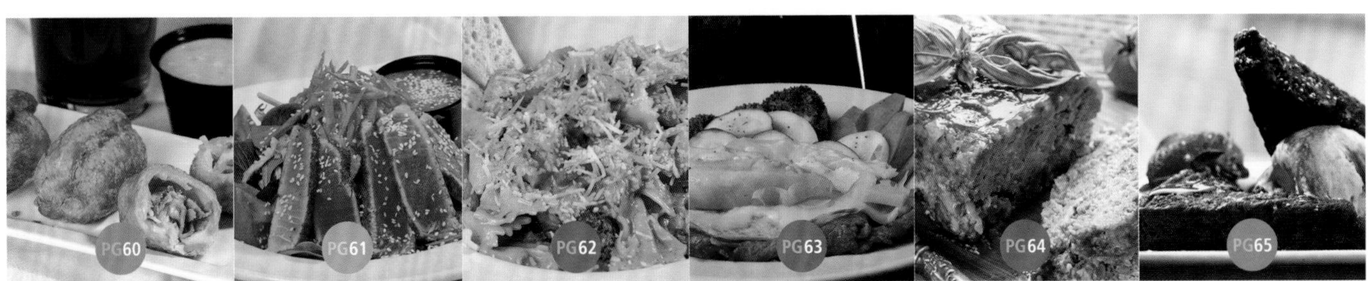

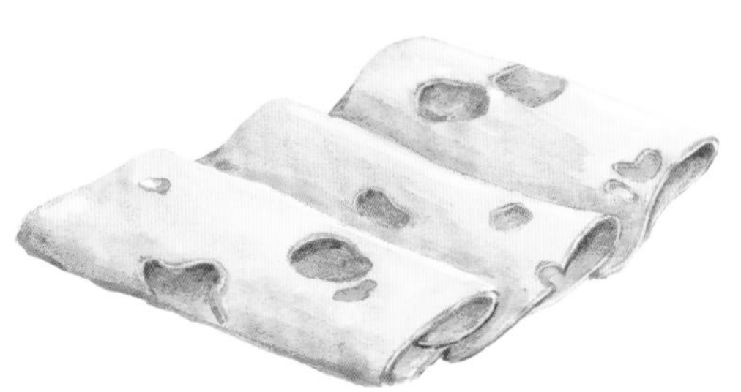

Reuben Rolls

PICKLING SPICE (for Pre-cured Cornbeef)
1 Tbsp whole allspice berries
1 Tbsp coriander seeds
1 Tbsp whole cloves
1 Tbsp whole mustard seeds
1 Tbsp red pepper flakes
1 Tbsp whole black peppercorns
6 large bay leaves
2 tsp ground ginger

4 2x3 inch puff pastry squares (available in either frozen sheets or fresh at the local market)
8 oz corned beef (purchase slices at deli counter or see recipe below)
2 oz sauerkraut
2 slices Swiss cheese

THOUSAND ISLAND SRIRACHA SAUCE
¼ cup chili sauce
¼ cup red wine vinegar
1 Tbsp Sriracha sauce (start with less and add more if you like)
2 Tbsp onion, finely minced
2 tsp dill pickle relish
1 garlic clove, minced
1 Tbsp fresh lemon juice
kosher salt to taste
freshly ground black pepper to taste

Reuben rolls are golden brown, house made, puff pastry rolls stuffed with seasoned corned beef, Swiss cheese and sauerkraut, and served with a spicy Thousand Island sauce on the side.

Thousand Island Sriracha Sauce

Blend together chili sauce, red wine vinegar, Sriracha sauce (available in local market), minced onion, dill pickle relish, garlic clove, lemon juice, and salt and pepper to taste.

Packaged Corned Beef

Packaged, already cured but uncooked brisket can be purchased at the local market and finished at home. Fill a large pot $^{2}/_{3}$ full with fresh water. Add all of the pickling spices to water. Bring to a boil. Reduce heat to a slow simmer, add brisket and cook for 3-4 hours until fork tender. (Check several times while cooking that water hasn't reduced too much – if needed, add additional fresh water to pot.) Cool and slice meat thinly against the grain.

Reuben Rolls

Place ½ slice of corned beef, along with 1 Tbsp of sauerkraut and a ½ slice of Swiss cheese in center of one pastry square. Roll tight. Fold down the ends of the roll and tuck in the edges. Flash fry for two minutes or until golden brown. Serve with the Sriracha Thousand Island dressing.

Serves 4

Note

Pickling spices often come with a cured brisket package. This package will give you quite a bit of corned beef. Multiply additional ingredients for larger parties to match corned beef quantity.

BEER PAIRING PARK CITY BREWERY Hooker Blonde Ale. Park City's Hooker Blonde ale takes its name from a fly fishing streamer commonly used on the many streams and rivers in northern Utah. It's the perfect beer for any sportsman or woman. It is brewed in a classic Kolsch style, crisp and light. A simple recipe that uses a single noble hop variety that adds zest to the pilsner malt base. Hooker Blonde Ale is thirst quenching and easy to drink.

Blackened Ahi Salad with Toasted Sesame Dressing

4 oz Ahi tuna steak
Chef Paul Prudhomme's
Magic Blend seasoning
4 oz mixed greens
½ cup carrots, shredded
¼ cup mandarin oranges
¼ cup grape tomatoes, halved
¼ cup roasted peanuts
1 cup crispy wonton strips

TOASTED SESAME DRESSING
1 Tbsp toasted sesame seeds
½ cup canola oil
6 Tbsp seasoned rice vinegar
4 Tbsp white sugar, or to taste
3 Tbsp sesame oil
2 Tbsp soy sauce (reduced sodium if desired)
1 garlic clove
1 tsp grated or minced ginger

WONTON STRIPS
1 package egg roll wraps
or wonton wrappers
vegetable, canola, or peanut oil

Ahi Tuna

Coat fish in Chef Paul Prudhomme's Magic Bend seasoning. Place Ahi steaks in a hot skillet to blacken, searing each side for only 10 seconds then let stand and cool. When cooled slice into four 1 oz pieces.

Toasted Sesame Dressing

To toast sesame seeds, spread out on a cookie sheet in the oven or toaster oven until lightly browned and aromatic. Be careful to watch them so that they don't burn.
Combine canola oil, seasoned rice vinegar, white sugar, (some like it sweeter with more sugar) sesame oil, soy sauce, garlic clove and half the toasted sesame seeds. Save the remaining seeds for garnish.

Wonton Strips

For homemade wonton strips cut egg roll or wonton wrappers into strips ¾ inch by 3 inches long.
In large skillet heat 1 inch of oil to around 360 degrees.
Fry cut strips in oil until golden brown then remove with slotted spoon and lay on paper towel to absorb excess oil.
Prepare quantity to your needs. Also these are a great side snack to salad.

Assembly

Shred carrots and combine with greens and mix well. Top greens and carrots with seared blackened Ahi Tuna. To finish, top with Mandarin oranges, grape tomatoes, and roasted peanuts. Drizzle with toasted sesame dressing, and then top with crispy wonton strips and toasted sesame seeds.

WINE PAIRING *CHARLES SMITH "Kung Fu Girl" Riesling (Columbia Valley, Washington) 2014.*
You can never go wrong with a Riesling and a Blackened Ahi Tuna. This Riesling will be perfect for this seafood delicacy. Right off the bat you will get crushed minerals on the palate. This then gives way to a bit of white peach, lime leaves, and Linden tree. The crushed stone echoes in the palate with a long, fresh finish. The sweetness of the fruit on this wine will give your mouth the perfect complement from the flavor of the seasoning.

Maddie Mae's Meatloaf*

¾ cup shallots, finely chopped
¾ cup scallions, finely chopped
½ cup carrots, finely chopped
½ cup celery, finely chopped
½ cup red bell pepper
3 Tbsp unsalted butter
2 tsp minced garlic
salt to taste
1 tsp freshly ground black pepper
½ tsp freshly ground white pepper

⅛ tsp cayenne pepper, for hotter
1 tsp ground cumin
½ tsp nutmeg, freshly grated
2 Tbsp fresh rosemary (optional)
3 eggs beaten
½ cup basil tomato sauce
½ cup ricotta cheese thinned with milk
2 lbs ground chuck, 85/15
¾ lb Italian sausage
¾ cup seasoned bread crumbs

BASIL TOMATO SAUCE
6 Tbsp olive oil
½ cup shallots, chopped
6 cloves garlic, minced
1 Tbsp sugar
one 28 oz can San Marzano tomatoes
pinch red pepper flakes
1 Tbsp lemon juice
salt and pepper to taste
10 basil leaves, chopped

Preheat oven to 375 degrees.

Meat Loaf

Finely chop shallots, scallions, carrots, celery and red bell pepper. Melt 3 Tbsp of unsalted butter, and sauté. Add salt and pepper to taste. Add garlic during the last few minutes to cook until moisture evaporates and are "happy." Set aside and let cool.

In a large bowl, combine cayenne pepper, ground cumin, nutmeg, rosemary, eggs, basil tomato sauce and ricotta cheese and mix well. Add ground chuck, Italian sausage, seasoned bread crumbs and sautéed vegetables. Mix well with hands, blending the spices, and vegetables completely with the ground meats.

Form a loaf in a baking dish, then place the baking dish into a larger dish partly filled with hot water. Bake at 375 degrees until done.

Basil Tomato Sauce

In a sauté pan on medium-low, heat olive oil. Add shallots and cook until translucent. Add minced garlic and cook until light brown. Add tomatoes, sugar, lemon juice, red pepper flakes, basil, and salt and pepper to taste. Simmer for 30 minutes. Let sauce cool. Then purée in blender or food processor.

Assembly

Reheat basil tomato sauce. Remove meatloaf from baking dish. Slice, plate and top with basil tomato sauce.

Serves 6

BOB CHRISTIE *PC Local, reformed banker, furniture maker, skier (of course) and purveyor of one of the best dining experiences in Park City. His favorite event is preparing Christmas dinner for his friends and family. He generously collaborated with Flanagans to create this Italian influenced meatloaf for his granddaughter Maddie Mae.*

**At Flanagan's ask for "The Meatloaf"*

WINE PAIRING *THE PRISONER COMPANY "Cabernet Blend" (Napa Valley, California) 2014.*
One of the most well known wine producers in California, The Prisoner Wine Co. had a great idea to combine Zinfandel with Cabernet Sauvignon, Syrah, Petite Syrah and Charbono, allowing for a wine with aromas of bing cherry, espresso, and a tad bit of roasted fig. Throughout the glass you will get a punch of ripe raspberries, pomegranate, and a few wild berries through this smooth and luscious wine.

Curried Chicken Pasta

2 cup bowtie pasta
1Tbsp butter
two 6 oz chicken breast
½ cup broccoli
½ cup zucchini, sliced
½ cup yellow squash, sliced
½ cup mushrooms, sliced
½ cup red peppers, sliced
salt and pepper to taste

CURRY SAUCE
4 Tbsp butter
1½ granny smith apples,
peeled and chopped
1 jumbo yellow onion, chopped
1½ tsp cumin
1½ tsp turmeric
½ cup curry powder
1 tsp kosher salt
¼ tsp cayenne pepper
2 cups heavy cream

Boil water and prepare bowtie pasta as directed.
In sauté pan, melt 1 Tbsp butter to coat pan and sauté chicken breast. Remove from pan and set aside.
Clean and break apart broccoli, slice zucchini, yellow squash, mushrooms and red peppers. Add vegetables to sauté pan. Add salt and pepper to taste and continue to sauté until vegetables are cooked but still firm.

Curry Sauce
In another sauté pan, add 4 Tbsp butter along with peeled and chopped apples and onions. Sweat apples and onions together until tender and translucent. Add cumin, turmeric, curry powder, kosher salt and cayenne pepper and mix thoroughly. Cook for 10 minutes. Add cream and bring to a boil. Cool, then place in blender and puree until smooth.
Yields approximately 1 qt so you will have plenty for the next recipe.

Tip
For milder curry sauce add less curry powder and less cayenne pepper. P.S. sauce is even better the next day.

Assembly
Mix together pasta, chicken and vegetables in large bowl, top with curry sauce and mix well.
Plate and enjoy.

WINE PAIRING *MER SOLEIL "Silver" (Central Coast, California) 2013. This unmistakable Chardonnay, bottled in a ceramic bottle, is the perfect pairing with Curry. It has a pale yellowish color and is fresh from start to finish. This wine, especially the 2013 vintage opens up with incredible aromas of fruit blossoms and Meyer lemon. Bright citrus shines through on the palate, with a crisp acidity and depth that truly brings out the wine's unoaked character.*

Corned Beef Boxty

5 oz corned beef
1 tsp garlic
1 pinch thyme
¼ wedge seasoned steamed cabbage
1 large russet potato
2 Tbsp butter
¼ cup milk

HORSERADISH CREAM
2 Tbsp prepared horseradish
1 Tbsp cider vinegar
1 tsp dry mustard
3 Tbsps mayonnaise
⅛ tsp ground red pepper
½ cup sour cream

BOXTY
1 cup dried potatoes
2 cups milk
3 qts cold water
4 cups white flour
3 eggs
4 medium russet potatoes, shredded
salt to taste

Homemade Boxty (potato crepe) with sliced and seasoned corned beef, apple onion relish, mashed potatoes, Swiss cheese, thyme, horseradish cream and seasoned cabbage.

Corned Beef and Mashed Potatoes

Sauté corned beef, apple onion relish, garlic and thyme.
Steam or sauté cabbage and set aside.
Peel and boil potato until cooked thoroughly. Transfer cooked potato to bowl and mash while slowly adding butter and milk to desired thickness.

Horseradish Cream

In a small bowl whisk together horseradish, vinegar, dry mustard, mayonnaise, red pepper and sour cream.

Boxty

In a large mixing bowl, combine dried potatoes, milk, and water. Mix on low speed, adding flour 4 cups at a time until thoroughly mixed.
In a separate bowl beat the eggs. Add beaten eggs to the dried potato flour mixture and continue to mix.
Peel and grate the raw potatoes and add to mix. Season with salt. Mix well. Use 8 oz. ladle and cook boxty as you would a crepe or pancake on a griddle until golden brown.

Assembly

Place ⅓ horseradish sauce on bottom of plate, and add boxty. Place ½ corned beef on top of boxty. Add mashed potatoes and cabbage, then fold boxty over. Put remainder of horseradish sauce on top.

Serves 4

BEER PAIRING *Wasatch Ghostrider White IPA 6% ABV. Legend has it the Ghostrider roams Utah's Wasatch Range seeking revenge: someone stole his White IPA recipe. Smooth and crisp, the pale barley and citrusy hops are a perfect complement to this rich salmon dish. It's too good to hide!*

THE BOXTY *is a traditional Irish potato pancake made from finely grated, potatoes and mashed potato and flour and milk. The boxty has become so popular it is now regularly seen in a variety of restaurant styles. Boxtys can be flavored with garlic and other spices for an added flavor. They can also be used as a wrap similar to tortillas for fajitas.*

Chocolate Salted Caramel Brownie

1 cup butter
1½ cup chocolate chips
1½ cup sugar
½ cup brown sugar
5 eggs (tempered)
2 tsp vanilla
1 tsp sea salt
2 tsp cocoa
1¼ flour
2 cups caramel

Flanagan's fudgy chocolate brownie square with sea salt and caramel drizzle served with a scoop of vanilla ice cream.

Preheat oven to 350 degrees.

In a large sauté pan melt butter, chocolate chips and sugars. In a separate bowl, temper five eggs by adding warm/hot water to the eggs without actually cooking the eggs. Add the vanilla, sea salt, cocoa and flour. Mix gently.

Fold in the caramel and the chocolate chips and sugar mixture. Pour onto 9x9 greased baking pan. Bake at 350 degrees for 20 minutes. Let cool and cut into squares.

Top with a scoop of your favorite vanilla ice cream.

BEER PAIRING *Creamy Guinness Stout.*
Everyone knows that one of the best beers the Irish drink is Guiness. This being the case what's chocolate and vanilla ice cream without the perfect beer pairing. Guinness is known for its rich flavor and creaminess. The distinctive black color and velvety finish gives this beer a harmonious experience with each sip. The palate will get a combination of flavors; sweet and bitter, as the malt arrives on cue to complement a base of roasted barley.

HYATT
CENTRIC™

HYATT CENTRIC™

EPC AT HYATT CENTRIC

CV

The Escala Provision Company, or EPC, is located in the AAA Four Diamond, ski-in/ski-out luxury Hyatt Centric Park City, a hotel located within Park City's Canyons Resort. EPC prides itself on providing an atmosphere that is casual and personal--the moment guests enter the lobby, they are greeted by Ellie the hotel dog, and the attentive staff encourages visitors to treat the hotel like a home. There is no division between the front and the back of the house, and the open kitchen invites diners to take a closer look or have a conversation with the chefs on their way to a cozy fireside table. The floor-to-ceiling windows in the dining room create an environment that integrates the landscape into the décor, and the honeycombed ceiling sculpture is a nod to Utah's pioneer past and moniker as the beehive state.

Executive Chef Nathan Larsen creates dishes using ingredients that represent the state of Utah, including duck, lamb, bison, and other game meats. "I use a lot of restraint when I cook," says Larsen, "rather than covering up the true flavors of the food with heavy sauces." Larsen also incorporates traditional cooking techniques like brining, curing, pickling, drying and smoking that are reminiscent of Utah's rich history and that are a new way for diners to experience unique flavors. These preservation methods focus on the artisanal side of cooking, altering the textures and imparting deeper essences. Menus change frequently, and shared plates are encouraged, allowing guests to sample more of the local region they came to explore. Friendly bartenders are happy to create signature cocktails or pair menu items with local wines, beers and spirits.

From the early settlers of Park City to today's savvy explorer, food is a language best served with great stories. EPC's menu is focused on community– the farming community at large where Chef Larsen sources his ingredients, and the community that he and the restaurant staff share it with. Servers bring dishes to the table with a story of where the food came from and how it was prepared, encouraging guests to create their own stories of memorable meals and unforgettable vacation experiences.

CHEF NATHAN LARSEN

After an early restaurant experience at Bangkok Thai and the New Yorker restaurants in NYC, Executive Chef Nathan Larsen attended the Culinary Institute of America near Hyde Park, New York. Upon graduating in 2002, Larsen moved back to Utah to work at Stein Eriksen Lodge's Glitretend restaurant. Three years later he returned to New York for a brief stint at the Peninsula Hotel. Larsen then joined the Hyatt Hotel family in Washington, DC, Phoenix and then on to Louisville, where he became the executive chef. When the Hyatt Centric Hotel opened at Park City's Canyons Village, he jumped at the chance to return to Utah. "I enjoy every single day of living here," he says. Larsen creates uncomplicated food using high quality ingredients and old-fashioned scratch cooking techniques.

PG72 PG73 PG74 PG75

HYATT
CENTRIC™

Whipped Goat Cheese with Black Pepper Caramel

PRESERVED LEMONS
8 ripe lemons
1 cup coarse kosher salt
1 cup sugar
1 cup fresh lemon juice
2 cups water

FLAT BREAD
2½ cups all-purpose flour
(plus a little extra for rolling)
1 tsp salt
½ tsp granulated sugar
⅔ cup water (plus additional if needed)
1 whole egg
3 Tbsp unsalted butter, melted, cooled slightly
2 tsp seeds (either pumpkin, poppy, sesame, etc)

GOAT CHEESE SPREAD
4 oz pckg cream cheese, softened
2 oz goat cheese, softened
¼ cup heavy cream
pinch of salt

BLACK PEPPER CARAMEL
1 cup packed brown sugar
½ cup half & half
4 Tbsp butter
pinch of salt
1 Tbsp vanilla extract
2 Tbsp cracked black pepper

Preserved Lemons

Wash lemons well and cut each into 8 wedges. With a sharp knife, score the lemon wedges in two or three places. Mix kosher salt and sugar together. In a shallow pan, sprinkle a bed of salt and sugar mix, and place lemons on top. Top with the remaining salt/sugar mixture and cover. Place in refrigerator for four days.
Remove lemon wedges from salt/sugar mixture and rinse with cool water. Place lemons in clean jar with water and lemon juice. Cover and place in refrigerator until ready to use. Preserved lemons will keep in refrigerator for 2-3 weeks.

Flat Bread

Preheat oven to 350 degrees. Place flour, salt and sugar in a medium bowl and whisk to combine. In a separate smaller bowl, whisk together water, egg and the melted butter. Add the egg mixture to the dry ingredients and stir until the dough comes together. Slowly add additional water if the dough is dry. Knead the dough in the bowl 5 or 6 times. Turn the dough out onto the counter and divide into 6 balls. Cover dough with a towel and allow to rest for 30 minutes. Roll out each dough ball on a pizza peel, (a flat surface to slide bread into oven), to desired thickness. Brush with honey and remaining butter, and top with seeds. Place in oven and bake until golden brown.

Goat Cheese Spread

Combine cream cheese, softened goat cheese, heavy cream and a pinch of salt in a food processor and pulse until combined. Add salt to taste.

Black Pepper Caramel

Mix the brown sugar, half & half, butter and salt in a saucepan over medium-low heat. Cook, whisking gently for 5-7 minutes until ingredients thicken. Add vanilla and cook another minute to thicken further. Turn off the heat and add the black pepper.

Assembly

Using an ice cream scoop, scoop goat cheese and place in shallow serving bowl. Spoon the black pepper caramel over the top. Garnish the top of the goat cheese with the preserved lemon. Serve with flat bread and enjoy!

Serves 4

HYATT CENTRIC™

Pickled Beet & Apple Salad with Apple Lemon Vinaigrette

PICKLED BEETS
4 medium sized beets, any color or variety
¼ cup salad oil, for beet rub
4 cups water
2 cups apple cider vinegar
1 cup sugar
1 tsp cloves
2 tsp fennel seed
1 tsp black pepper
1 tsp mustard seed
2 bay leaves
salt to taste

APPLE LEMON VINAIGRETTE
1 oz apple juice
1 tsp Dijon mustard
2 Tbsp cider vinegar
¼ tsp salt
2 tsp sugar
½ tsp lemon juice
1 clove garlic, minced
1 Tbsp minced shallot
1 Tbsp chopped green onion
2 tsp olive oil
salt and pepper
blue cheese crumbles

Preheat oven to 350 degrees.

Pickled Beets

Clean beets in cool water with rag to remove any dirt. Rub the beets with the oil and place in shallow pan. Cover pan with plastic wrap and a top layer of aluminum foil. Bake in 350 degree oven for one hour or until a knife can be inserted easily into the center of the beet. Remove beets from pan and allow to cool. Remove the skins and dice.

In a large saucepan, combine water apple cider vinegar, sugar, cloves, fennel, black pepper, mustard seed, bay leaves and salt. Simmer for five minutes until all sugar and salt is dissolved. Strain into a clean container and cool. Add beets to cooled pickling liquid and refrigerate for 2-3 days.

Apple Lemon Vinaigrette

Combine apple juice, Dijon mustard, cider vinegar, sugar, lemon juice, minced garlic, minced shallot, and chopped green onions in food processor and blend until smooth. Drizzle in the olive oil and season with salt and pepper.

Garnish

Toast ¼ cup pine nuts and allow to cool. Place cooled pine nuts and salt in food processor and pulse until crumbled.

Assembly

Place mixed greens in bowl and toss with Apple Lemon Vinaigrette. Put one serving of greens on each plate. Arrange beets, sliced apples and blue cheese crumbles on top. Sprinkle with pine nuts.

Serves 6-8

HYATT
CENTRIC™

Pan Seared Trout with Fingerling Potato Hash & Warm Bacon Vinaigrette

4 trout fillets cut in half
salt and pepper
1 Tbsp cooking oil

FINGERLING POTATO HASH
1 lb Fingerling potatoes, cut and steamed
3 cloves garlic, sliced
1 shallot, sliced
2 Tbsp salad oil

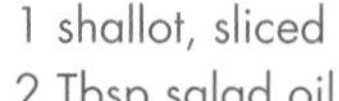

HOUSE CURED BACON
3 Tbsp salt
2 Tbsp brown sugar
1 tsp black peppercorns
1 Tbsp red pepper flakes
1 tsp mustard seed, crushed
1 tsp fennel seed
1 lb pork belly

BACON DRESSING
4 thick-cut slices of bacon, diced
3 Tbsp Dijon mustard
2 Tbsp brown sugar
1 medium shallot, diced
3 garlic cloves, chopped
½ tsp salt
½ tsp ground white pepper
¼ cup balsamic vinegar

Salt Cure Mixture
Whisk salt, brown sugar, black peppercorns, red pepper flakes, mustard seed and fennel together (can be made ahead and stored covered in dry location for up to one month).

House Cured Bacon
Lightly rinse pork belly with cold water and dry uncovered. Lay pork belly on a baking tray with a wire rack. Rub both sides of pork belly with salt cure mixture. Cover with plastic wrap and refrigerate for three days. Remove pork belly from cure and rinse off excess. Place in smoker with Mesquite or Applewood chips, and smoke for 1½ hours. Remove from smoker and cool. Cut amount needed for recipe and freeze remaining bacon for later use.

Fingerling Potato Hash
Cut and steam Fingerling potatoes. Combine potatoes with sliced garlic cloves and sliced shallot. Coat medium sauce pan with oil and cook over medium heat until potatoes are golden brown.

Trout
Lay trout fillets on plate or sheet pan, flesh side down. Pat skin dry with paper towel, then season with salt and pepper. Heat oil in non-stick pan over medium heat. Place trout in pan, skin side down. Cook for three minutes, then flip and cook three minutes longer. Remove from heat and keep warm.

Bacon Dressing
In a frying pan, heat diced bacon over medium heat until crisp. Remove from pan and set aside. Add mustard, brown sugar, shallot, garlic, salt and pepper to warm bacon drippings and whisk to combine. Add vinegar and whisk to combine until vinaigrette thickens. Add cooked bacon and stir. Remove from heat and spoon over trout dish.

Assembly
Heat fingerling potato hash. In a small pan, heat 3 tablespoons of bacon vinaigrette dressing over low heat. Place a portion of hash on each plate and top with trout fillet. Spoon bacon vinaigrette dressing over trout and garnish with citrus segments.

Serves 4

HYATT CENTRIC™

Warm Banana Bread with Chocolate Banana Ice Cream & Caramelized Honey

CHOCOLATE BANANA ICE CREAM
4 ripe bananas
3 Tbsp creamy peanut butter
1½ tsp unsweetened cocoa powder
½ cup heavy cream
½ tsp vanilla extract

BANANA BREAD
2 cups flour
1 tsp baking soda
¼ tsp salt
⅔ cup butter
¾ cup brown sugar
2 eggs
2½ cups mashed overripe bananas

CARAMELIZED BANANA AND HONEY
½ cup honey
1 Tbsp butter
2 bananas, peeled and cut in half lengthwise, then quartered
2 Tbsp brown sugar

Preheat oven to 350 degrees.

Chocolate Banana Ice Cream

Combine bananas, creamy peanut butter, unsweetened cocoa powder, heavy cream and vanilla extract in food processor and pulse until combined. Freeze until ready to use.

Banana Bread

Lightly grease and flour a loaf pan.
In a large bowl, combine flour, baking soda and salt.
In a separate bowl, cream together butter and brown sugar. Stir in eggs and mashed bananas until well blended. Add banana mixture to bowl of flour mixture and stir lightly to moisten.

Pour batter into prepared loaf pan and bake at 350 degrees for 45-50 minutes.

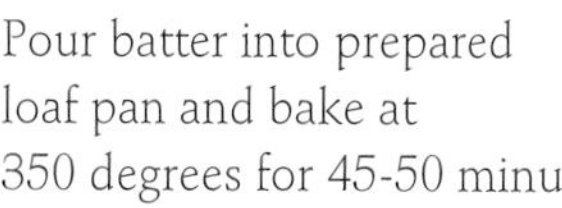

Caramelized Honey

In small saucepan, add honey and heat over medium low heat until consistency of caramel.

Caramelized Banana

Melt butter in pan over medium heat. Add brown sugar and cook until sugar is melted. Add bananas and cook until caramelized.

Assembly

Melt butter in a nonstick pan over medium high heat.
Cut banana bread into 1 inch slices, add to pan and brown on both sides. Place banana bread slices in serving bowls.
Top with caramelized bananas, one scoop of chocolate ice cream. Drizzle with caramelized honey.

J&G
GRILL

J&G GRILL

DV

Located at the top of the funicular at The St. Regis Deer Valley, J&G Grill is a worldly delight. The restaurant combines a curated selection of celebrity chef Jean-Georges Vongerichten's greatest appetizers, side dishes and accompaniments from his portfolio of domestic and international restaurants around the world. Simply grilled preparations accompanied by bold condiments anchor the J&G Grill dining experience, while seamless service, intriguing wines, brews and specialty cocktails complement it all.

At every opportunity, Chef Rachel Wiener incorporates the highest quality, locally-sourced ingredients to create menus that are rooted in the principles of slow-cooked, ranch-to-table fare. "At the resort, our facilities are state-of-the-art and we have incredible access to a variety of local ranches that allow us to deliver award-winning dishes to our diners. Whether it's local Koosharem Trout, elk or other produce, we love providing our guests with innovative dishes that utilize the finest ingredients Utah has to offer."

Enhancing the enthusiastic fare are noteworthy surroundings: the dining room boasts a captivating exhibition kitchen, double-sided wood-burning fireplace, walls clad in quartz stone and a ceiling framed with walnut ceruse beams. For a more intimate dining experience, the Wine Vault boasts a 13,000 bottle collection, housing the largest wine list in Utah. The atmosphere is rivaled only by the magnificent slopeside views that beckon from beyond the floor-to-ceiling windows.

J&G Grill is open for breakfast, lunch, and dinner daily.

CHEF RACHEL WEINER

Chef Rachel Wiener serves as Executive Sous Chef and Chef de Cuisine at J&G Grill, overseeing menu planning for the restaurant, award-winning wine dinners and the St. Regis Bar.

Chef Wiener's passion for food comes from growing up in a Hungarian and Indian household with parents who loved to cook. Throughout her life, she was exposed to a variety of exotic flavors and dishes that inspired her to pursue a career as a chef.

A desire to further her career while also enjoying the breathtaking scenery and mountain lifestyle led her to The St. Regis Deer Valley. Though still learning to ski, Chef Rachel has become an expert at après ski, and you can often find her fireside with a glass of Oban scotch or a cold beer.

House Made Burrata, Citrus salad

MOZZARELLA
3½ cups curd, broken into 1inch pieces
½ cup salt
4 qts hot water

RICOTTA MIX
1½ cups fresh Ricotta
¼ cup heavy cream

BURRATA
⅓ cup mozzarella, stretched smooth,
¼ inch thick, draped into a coffee cup
3 Tbsp ricotta mix

BASIL MIX
1 Tbsp micro basil
2 Tbsp Frantoia evo olive oil
¼ tsp green Thai chili, chopped fine
1 tsp salt
pinch of ground fennel

CITRUS
12 cara cara orange, segmented
12 clementine, peeled by hand and pulled apart into un-broken segments
12 pink grapefruit, segments, cut in ½
Maldon sea salt
coarse black pepper
olive oil

Mozzarella

Put curd in a large bowl. Put salt in a 2 quart lexon and fill with hot water. Immediately pour over curd and let sit for 5 minutes. Gather ⅓ cup worth of curd and work gently until smooth and shiny, then stretch into a ¼ inch thick disk and drape in an espresso cup.

Ricotta Mix

In a large bowl add fresh Ricotta and heavy cream and mix well.

Burrata

Spoon the ricotta into the center of the mozzarella and pull all the sides together to make a package. Squeeze the end to pinch it closed and squeeze off the loose excess end. Put in a container of cool (not cold) water.
As needed, temper cheese to room temperature;
(either in batches before service or microwave in
5 second pulses as needed).

Basil Mix

Combine Frantoia evo olive oil, green Thai chili, salt and ground fennel seed. Chop Thai basil and mix. Prepare in batches so the basil stays fresh.

Assembly

Arrange citrus segments on the bottom of the platter, top with burrata balls and season liberally with Maldon salt and black pepper. Garnish each burrata ball with the basil mix, then drizzle olive oil over everything.

Makes 9-10 Burrata balls.

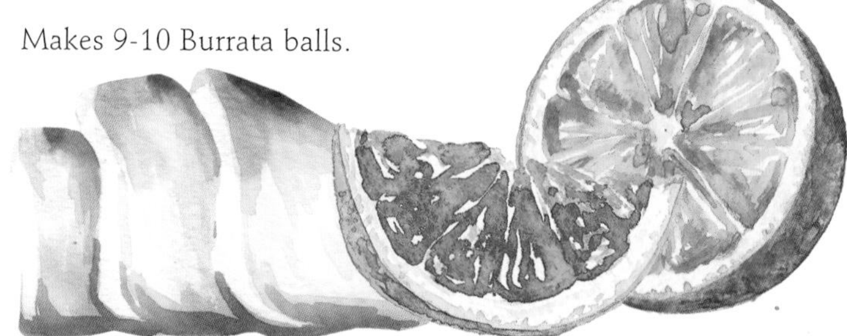

WINE PAIRING *PASCAL JOLIVET, Sancerre, (Sancerre, France), 2013. Sancerre wines are derived from three soil types- flint, limestone and clay- which provide beautiful minerality and aromas of lime zest and fresh cut honeydew melon.*

Tuna Tartar, Avocado, Spicy Radish & Ginger Marinade

TUNA
1 cup large ground tuna
1½ Tbsp olive oil
pinch Thai chili minced
¾ tsp salt
4 tsp shallot, minced

CHILI OIL
⅛ cup ancho chili, seeds removed & toasted
¾ tsp dried chipotle, seeds removed & toasted
⅛ tsp allspice berries toasted
⅛ tsp cloves toasted
1½ Tbsp fennel seeds, toasted
1 Tbsp mace, toasted
1 Tbsp star anise, toasted
2½ tsp cinnamon sticks, toasted
1½ Tbsp salt
6 cups grape seed oil

KAFFIR SYRUP
1 cup lime juice
1 cup sugar
⅛ cup Kaffir lime leaves,
washed and chopped

GINGER MARINADE
½ cup ginger
⅛ cup olive oil
¾ cup Champagne vinegar
¾ cup Soy sauce
⅓ cup Kaffir syrup

AVOCADO
3 Tbsp ripe avocado mash
1 tsp olive oil

12-15 slices radishes

Tuna

In a mixing bowl toss tuna with olive oil, then gently season with salt, minced shallot and minced Thai chili. Keep in bowl over ice.

Chili Oil

Remove seeds from ancho chilies and the dried chipotle and place on baking sheet. Add allspice berries, cloves, fennel seeds, mace, Star anise, cinnamon sticks, and salt, and toast all in oven.
Put in a blender and puree medium fine. Combine with the grapeseed oil in a sauté pan and heat, stirring, until oil reaches 160 degrees.
Let cool. Strain through chinois and push for total extraction.

Kaffir Syrup

Combine lime juice, sugar, and Kaffir lime leaves in a pot and heat to 190 degrees. Remove from stove then steep, covered, until cool.

Ginger Marinade

Peel ginger and rough chop. Puree in blender with olive oil, until totally smooth. Mix champagne vinegar, soy sauce and Kaffir syrup.

Assembly

Mash ripe avocados with olive oil and season with salt. Place a 3 inch ring mold into the center of a cold appetizer bowl and spoon the avocado into the bottom of the mold. Top with the tuna tartar. Shingle the radishes on top. Unmold the tartar and ladle 3 oz ginger marinade into the bowl. Drizzle with the chili oil.

Serves 2.

WINE PAIRING *NV BILLECART-SALMON Brut Rose Ay, Champagne. This Champagne is light and delicate with elegant bubbles providing lift and structure from fine Pinot Noir tannins.*

Sauteed Halibut with Corn, Chanterelles and Silky Carrot

FISH
4 lbs halibut
salt, pinch
white pepper, pinch
extra virgin olive oil

FENNEL-ROSEMARY TEA
1 ½ cups fennel scraps, chopped
¾ cup corn cobs, cut into 1" pieces
1 ¾ Tbsp rosemary sprigs, broken last minute
5 cups tea water
1 ¾ Tbsp salt

CORN-CHANTERELLES
1 ⅓ cups corn kernels
1 cup chanterelles, washed, trimmed, cut in ½ or ¼'s depending on size
2 tsp extra virgin olive oil
⅛ tsp salt
1 ½ tsp garlic, sliced very thin
½ cup extra virgin olive oil
½ cup fennel, small dice
1 Tbsp red finger chili, seeded, brunoise cut
2¾ fennel tea
½ tsp salt
¼ cup fresh lemon juice

CARROT PUREE
1 ¾ cups carrot, peeled and sliced thin
1 cup water
2 tsp salt
1 ½ Tbsp sugar
2 Tbsp butter

GARNISH
chervil, picked

Fennel-Rosemary Tea
In a quart container, combine fennel, corn and rosemary. Add tea water and cover for 30 minutes. Strain through a chinois, pushing for total extraction (you should have 5 cups of liquid). Season with the salt.

Corn-Chanterelle
Combine corn kernels, chanterelles, and extra virgin olive oil and mix well. Char in a smoking hot pan to achieve a light smoky flavor. Transfer to a container and set aside until needed.

In a medium size sauce pot, cook garlic in olive oil until tender and very pale golden. Add fennel and cook on low heat, covered, until tender. Add the corn-chanterelle mix and the chili and sauté to combine. Add fennel tea and bring to a simmer. Remove from heat and season with the salt and lemon juice.

Carrot Puree
Combine sliced carrots, water, salt, sugar, and butter and cook covered on high heat until carrots are completely tender. Puree all in blender until totally smooth.

Halibut
In sauté pan heat olive oil over medium-high heat, sear halibut flesh side down. Flip halibut and finish cooking until golden brown.

Assembly
Spoon the carrot puree into the center of a warm plate. Warm the corn mix on low heat until hot all the way through. Spoon the corn mix liberally around puree and garnish with some chervil leaves. Place fish on top of carrot puree and serve.

WINE PAIRING BUISSON-CHARLES Chablis Grand Cru Vaudesir (Chablis, France) 2013. *Chardonnay from Chablis is crisp and high in acid due to a cool climate. This wine has notes of flint, Asian pear and fresh-picked white flowers.*

Caramelized Lamb Chops and Roasted Brussels Sprouts, Pecans and Avocado

BRUSSELS SPROUTS (serves 1 portion)
extra virgin olive oil, as needed
1¼ cup Brussels sprouts, trimmed, blanched, shocked, cut in ½
salt and black pepper
1 tsp thyme leaves
¼ cup pecans, toasted, cut in half
1 avocado, small dice

MUSTARD BUTTER
1 cup soft butter
⅓ cup whole grain mustard
⅓ cup Dijon mustard
1¾ Tbsp mustard oil
1 Tbsp lime zest
2 Tbsp fresh lime juice
½ Tbsp fleur de sel

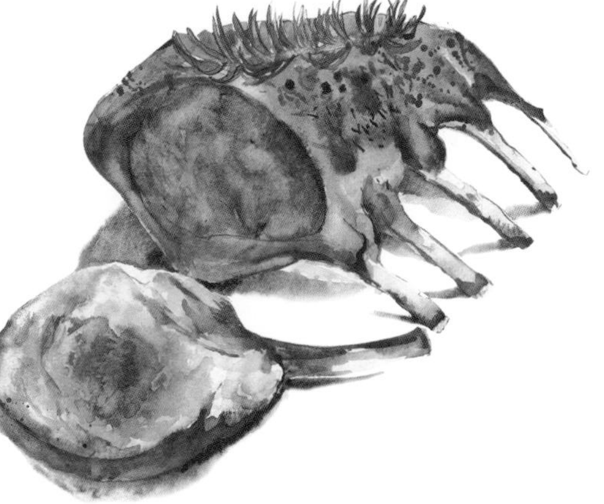

LAMB
1 lamb rack
salt to taste
pinch allepo chili powder
grapeseed oil as needed
1 tsp butter
1 garlic clove
1 sprig thyme

GARNISH
fleur de sel
Chives, minced

Brussels Sprouts
Heat a sauté pan with olive oil until smoking and add brussel sprouts. Season with salt and pepper and cook until crispy. Add thyme, pecans and avocado and toss gently to warm.

Mustard Butter
Combine butter, whole grain mustard, Dijon mustard, mustard oil, lime zest, fresh lime juice and fleur de sel and mix well. Roll into plastic wrap tubes 2 inches in diameter. Refrigerate until needed.

Lamb
Season lamb with salt and chili powder. Roast in a hot pan with grape seed oil until lamb is well caramelized and cooked to temperature. Finish with butter, garlic and thyme and baste until fragrant.

Assembly
Arrange Brussels sprouts neatly in the center of a hot plate. Place lamb chops on sprouts and top with a ½" thick slice of the mustard butter. Sprinkle with chives and fleur de sel.

WINE PAIRING CASANOVA DI NERI 'Tenuta Nuova' Brunello di Montalcino (Montalcino, Italy) 2013.
This wine offers bright and tart fruit with aromas of Bing cherry and fresh sawn wood. Brunello means "little brown one" and is composed of 100 percent Sangiovese.

Lavender Scented Pound Cake, Macerated Strawberries, Ricotta Ice Cream

DV | D

RICOTTA ICE CREAM
2 cups cream
1 cup milk
1 cup sugar
8 yolks
1 cups Ricotta
1 oz rum
¾ tsp Salt
½ lemon, finely zested & juiced

POUND CAKE
½ lb butter, diced, not too cold
3 cups sugar (flavor with lavender for 24 hours then tamis)
1 Tbsp fresh lavender, optional
6 eggs, room temperature
9 oz cake flour
½ tsp salt
1 tsp baking powder
8 oz Cream
2 tsp vanilla extract
½ lemon, juice and zest

LAVENDER SYRUP
1 cup sugar
¾ cup water
½ vanilla bean split
1 oz lavender flowers

MACERATED STRAWBERRIES
2 cups fresh strawberries, stemmed and cut into ¼'s
3 Tbsp sugar

Ricotta Ice Cream

Bring cream, milk and half the sugar to a full boil. Slowly add yolks (to temper in yolks) and remaining sugar. Pass through a fine mesh sieve. Stir in remaining ingredients and cool in water bath.

Pound Cake

Cream butter and sugar until light and fluffy, approximately 5 minutes. Slowly add eggs two at a time, scraping bowl often. Sift flour, salt and baking powder, then add half of it. Add in the cream, vanilla, lemon juice and zest, and lavender, and finish with remaining dry flour mixture. Do not over mix. Divide between four buttered floured loaf pans. Sprinkle the top with sugar and bake at 310 degrees for approximately 45-60 minutes. When cooled, cut end off of loaves, and cut into 9 slices.

Lavender Syrup

Heat the sugar and water and reduce to syrup. Add vanilla beans and flowers and cool.

Macerated Strawberries

Toss and let macerate for a minimum of 20 minutes.

Assembly

Put a portion of strawberries onto a plate, top with a slice of pound cake, then more strawberries, another slice, then finish with strawberries. Put a quenelle of ice cream onto plate. Drizzle with lavender syrup.

Serves 8.

WINE PAIRING MASSIMO ROMEO ESTATES DOC Vin Santo di Montepulciano (Montalcino, Italy) 1997.

Vin Santo wine offers beautiful notes of honey, dried fruit and almond which gains depth and character from extended oak barrel aging.

·The Dueling Piano Experience·
Fine Dining in a Pub Atmosphere · Family Friendly Restaurant · 14 Scotches 21 Whiskeys And More
Molly Blooms
A Gastro Pub
EST. 2009
· Gourmet Burgers and Craft Droughts at 7,000 Feet in Elevation · Traditional Irish Fare and Lovely Ladies in Kilts
·Kimball Junction, Park City, UT·

MOLLY BLOOMS

KJ

A Gastropub is a British term for a public house that serves high-quality fare. And, of course, a "public house" is a pub. While you will find great bar food at Molly Blooms, you will also be delighted by our gourmet comfort cuisine offerings. Molly Blooms offers the best fish & chips in Utah, shepherd's pie, steaks, seafood, gourmet salads, house made soups and so much more. Just like the pubs in Ireland, Molly Blooms is a family friendly place where the young ones are always welcome.

Molly Blooms Gastropub opened for Saint Patrick's Day 2009 and has been a local go-to ever since. We are located in Kimball Junction just east of Smiths Grocery Store. With plentiful parking and multiple bus stops within a minute or two walk, you can find and get to us with ease. While St. Patrick's Day is special for us and our regulars, we make sure to treat our guests with fantastic service and delightful cuisine in our relaxed casual pub atmosphere everyday. Live music is a staple of pubs in Ireland, and Molly Blooms Gastropub is no different. On the weekends we feature a high energy, all request Dueling Piano Show (with a gong), and singer songwriters and jazz throughout the week. If you're lucky, you'll come in during one of the youth music concerts we regularly host. Performances are by the Ecker Hill Middle School String Band, Park City Rockers and Music Garage.

In Utah, liquor regulations are a little strange but no worries! At Molly Blooms we offer an excellent selection of spirits, wines and brews. Beers are available both in the bottle and off the tap. Our "coffin box" has 16 fine local and traditional brands.

"Craic" or "crack," is a term for news, gossip, fun, entertainment, and enjoyable conversation, particularly prominent in Ireland. Starting from the friendly welcoming service, through the great entertainment and excellent food and drink, you'll find it at Molly Blooms.

CHEF GREGG DAVISON

Restaurateur and Chef Gregg Davison grew up in Danbury, Connecticut and has been in restaurants since 1990. With extensive experience in short order grilling and casual dining, he envisioned Molly Blooms as a comfort food haven with a gastropub flare. The original single menu design was a collaborative effort with friends Chef Brett Miltenburger, Chef Justin Howell and Kim Wessel-Howell.

With lunch, dinner, brunch, late night menus and three seasons of menu changes, Chef Davison takes advantage of the seasonal fruits and vegetables which have become a staple of the gastronomical offerings at Molly Blooms. Customers unfamiliar with gastropubs are in for a treat with the savory and approachable comfort themed cuisine, including the "Best fish & Chips" in Utah, according to City Weekly readers' poll.

Molly Malones Cockle and Mussel Chowder "A St Patrick's Day Tradition"

2 Tbsp olive oil
4 pieces of bacon, minced
2 Tbsp butter
1 leek, minced
1 medium carrot, minced
1 medium potato, skin on, minced

2 lbs mixed cockles, clams and mussels
1 ½ cups Pinot Grigio or other white wine
1 ½ cups light or heavy cream
salt and freshly ground black pepper
4 Tbsp coarsely chopped fresh parsley

ROUX
4 Tbsp butter
4 Tbsp flour

Clean and rinse mussels and clams. In stock pot, over medium heat melt butter and sauté the bacon until soft. Add minced leek, carrot and potato and continue to sauté until light brown. Add the white wine and cleaned mussels and clams. Cook until the clams and mussels open up. Discard any that remain closed. Add the cream and simmer for 5 minutes or until the potatoes are soft.

In a separate pan, melt remaining butter. Slowly add the flour, stirring constantly to combine and form a thick roux. Turn off the heat so as not to burn.

Thicken the stock with the roux two tablespoon at a time until a light chowder consistency is reached.
Add the parsley and season with salt and pepper to taste.
Served with hand-torn French bread.

Serves 4 to 6

BEER PAIRING *Creamy Guinness Stout.*
Everyone knows that one of the best beers the Irish drink is Guiness. This being the case, what's a St. Patricks Day soup without the perfect beer pairing. Guinness is known for its rich flavor and creaminess. The distinctive black color and velvety finish gives this beer a harmonious experience with each sip. The palate will get a combination of flavors; sweet and bitter, as the malt arrives on cue to complement a base of roasted barley.

Summer Salad

KJ | S

MUSTARD VINAIGRETTE
⅓ cup white wine vinegar
1 tsp mustard (any kind will do)
Pinch of salt and pepper
½ Tbs fresh red onion or shallot, minced
⅓ cup of olive oil

¼ loaf of French bread baguette
asparagus bunch
2 medium tomatoes (any variety)

1 bowl of mixed lettuces of your choice
or
1 bag of high quality spring mix with kale, spinach, and frisee, or collect your own mix at the market.

Low Calorie Mustard Vinaigrette

Pour white vinegar into a blender. Add mustard, salt and pepper and minced red onion or shallot. Blend on low, slowly adding oil. This will yield about ¾ cup of emulsified dressing. Excess can be kept covered in the refrigerator for a week.

Salad

Grill 2 large or 4 small asparagus per serving. Grill 2 slices or wedges of tomato per salad. For grilling both the asparagus and tomato, a broiler can be used instead of the grill.
Slice French baguette at an angle ¼ inch thick. Toast slices and brush lightly with butter or olive oil.

Assembly

In large bowl toss salad with mustard vinaigrette dressing. Plate individual salads and add the grilled asparagus and toasted French bread.

Serves 4.

WINE PAIRING *Marchese Antinori Cuvée Royale (FRANCIACORTA, LOMBARDY, ITALY) N/V.*
In Italy sparkling wines are not considered Champagne, Champagne is only called that when it's from that region in France. Antinori, however, does a brilliant job at creating the perfect sparkling substitution. This light straw yellow wine gives you a creamy and bubbling flavor blast that shows notes of white peaches and bread, on its nose. The flavors stay alive and fruitful throughout each sip. Perfect to pair with this salad.

Rack of Lamb, with Garlic Mashers, Vegetable Medley and Cucumber Mint Relish

2 racks of Lamb, preferable New Zealand
salt and pepper
olive oil

MASHED POTATOES
4 large potatoes, skin on
¼ cup of cream or milk
1 stick of butter
½ tsp granulated garlic
salt and pepper to taste

VEGETABLE MEDLEY
2 Tbsp olive oil
2 squash, jullienned
2 zucchini, jullienned
¼ red onion
2 carrots, jullienned
¼ cup string beans
salt and pepper

CUCUMBER MINT RELISH
1 cucumber, diced, seeds removed
2 Tbsp fresh mint
2 Tbsp olive oil
¼ tsp cumin powder
¼ tsp cayenne pepper
salt and peppler

Lamb Rack

Cut lamb into individual pieces and trim as needed. Toss in a small mixing bowl with olive oil and salt and pepper. Grill or broil to medium rare. Finish in oven at 350 degrees for a more well done temperature.

Mashed Potatoes

Cube potatoes and boil vigorously for 20 minutes or until soft. Whip with butter, cream, garlic and salt in a table top mixer.

Vegetable Medley

Sauté or steam julienned squash, zucchini, red onion, carrot and green beans with a little olive oil and salt and pepper until soft, 3-5 minutes.

Cucumber mint relish

In a small bowl combine fresh, diced cucumber, mint, olive oil, cumin, salt and pepper and cayenne pepper. Can be refrigerated covered for 3 days.

Serves 4

WINE PAIRING *Domaine Serene "Evanstad" Pinot Noir (Willamette Valley, Oregon) 2012.*
One of the first Pinot Noirs I have ever had. This one has a special place in my heart with flavors like cherry, toffee, and raspberry on the nose. This transforms into a well-structured glass of bright crisp red & black cherries, The finish delivers a bit of oak that leaves the mouth wanting more. Lamb and an Oregon Pinot are always a perfect pairing; I highly recommend this one.

Whiskey Bread Pudding with Ice Cream

1 doz brioche rolls, hand shredded
4 eggs, beaten
1 ½ cups cream
1 ½ cups sugar
1 ½ tsp cinnamon
2 oz Irish whiskey

Pre-heat oven to 350 degrees

Shred the brioche rolls by hand.
In a large mixing bowl beat the eggs and then add in the shredded brioche rolls, cream, sugar, cinnamon and whiskey and mix thoroughly.

Transfer mixture to a greased 9 X 9 baking pan.
Bake for 25 minutes.

Serve hot or can be refrigerated and reheated for service.
Plate individually with a scoop of your favorite vanilla ice cream and a light dusting of cinnamon or nutmeg.

Serves 8.

WINE PAIRING *What else do you pair with a whiskey bread pudding? An Irish coffee of course. Grab a cup of your favorite coffee, throw in a shot, or two, of Jameson or your favorite Irish whiskey, and top it off with a nice sized dollop of freshly whipped cream.*

The Mulligan Lemonatta

2 lemons cut into thick wheels, 8 pieces total
1 Tbsp candied ginger
6 oz Jameson whisky
6 oz Jameson Black whisky
4 cans of Pellegrino Lemonata soda

Grill or broil all 8 pieces of lemon.

In a glass bowl or tumbler, muddle together the candied ginger, 4 pieces of grilled lemon and the whisky.

Strain the muddled mixture and pour equal portions of the liquid over ice into 4 mason jars.
Top off the mason jars with Pellegrino Lemonatta soda.
Garnish with the remaining wheel of lemon.
Refrigerate.

Serves 4

The Mulligan Lemonatta is zesty and lemony wiht a bit of a kick. Lemonatta is a real thirst quenching cocktail.

MUDDLE *by pressing the ingredients against the side of a glass with a muddler. When using fresh herbs and fruits for cocktails, muddling is a method to blend in the flavors of the item into the cocktail. By doing this it releases the flavors so they bind better with the alcohol. For heartier firmer herbs and ingredients, a strong hand is used to muddle ingredients but for more delicate herbs use a lighter touch to avoid a bitter flavor release.*

TEAM
SALT LAKE 2002

The Mustang
MUSTANG
890
THE SHOPS AT
The Village

The Mustang

THE MUSTANG

MS

Dustin Stein, owner and General Manager of The Mustang, is a Park City local who sparked his passion for the restaurant industry at the young age of 15 when he bussed tables at Grub Steak restaurant while attending Park City High School. He went on to graduate from the University of Utah with a degree in finance. After graduating, and following a few years as a golf pro, he returned to his undeniable passion in the hospitality industry. Dustin's drive for excellence led him back to Park City where his customer service skills propelled him to the highest levels of the industry, including Food & Beverage Manager at the 5-star world-renowned Stein Eriksen Lodge.

Dustin worked at The Mustang for several years before he became the proud owner in 2015. On the Main Street scene since 2004, The Mustang restaurant has continually been ranked as one of the top dining experiences in a mountain town known around the world for its first class dining. Dustin encourages his staff to bring their own personalities and passion for Park City to every table.The perfect pairing of friendly professional service and exquisite cuisine keeps The Mustang at the top. While working together at the Stein Eriksen Lodge, Dustin recognized the talent in the young and upcoming Chef Edgar Gonzalez and recruited him for a new era at The Mustang. Together they have incorporated classic house favorite dishes with their own flare of flavors and artistic presentation.

The Mustang is known for having one of the largest fresh fish selections on Main Street, including their Utah Red Trout awarded "Best Fish Dish" by City Weekly. On their eclectic menu featuring a range of items from the Duck Chile Relleno to the Shrimp Potstickers, there is something for every taste-bud. Of course, no meal is complete without the delectable signature chocolate souffle.

Relax in a beautiful mountain setting on their expansive patio on historic lower main street. It's the perfect location to watch bands and parades during Park City's many summertime events. In the winter, enjoy the large fire pit, or head inside where you will find contemporary art from local and new artists. The newly remodeled bar features many of Utah's very own spirits and brews.

CHEF EDGAR GONZALEZ

In 2015, Chef Edgar Gonzalez and Dustin Stein teamed up to create the new Mustang restaurant.

Native to Michoacan, Mexico, Edgar came to the US with his mother and brother when he was eleven. Practically penniless and settling in the small town of Ephraim, his mother saved enough money to buy ingredients to make salsa for sale. Edgar watched as his mother sold mole, posole, tamales and other Mexican dishes on her days off. He's had a passion for food ever since.

A graduate of Park City High School, Edgar attended Le Cordon Bleu College of Culinary Arts in Las Vegas. During college, he worked at a private catering company with Chef Salvati. Moving back to Park City, he worked with Executive Chefs Zane Holmquist *(cont'd on page 102)*

Asian Shrimp Potstickers

1 package eggroll skins

FILLING
4 cups finely chopped shrimp
1 tsp olive oil
pinch of salt and pepper
½ cup green onions, chopped

SAUCE
1 cup soy sauce
1 cup white vinegar
1 oz water
1 Tbsp sesame oil
1 tsp crushed red chili peppers
1 tsp minced garlic
1 Tbsp sugar

Filling

Mix together finely chopped shrimp, olive oil, pinch of salt and pepper and chopped green onions.

Sauce

In a separate bowl mix soy sauce, white vinegar, water, sesame oil, crushed red chili peppers, minced garlic, and sugar and set aside.

Fill eggroll skins with 1 oz of potsticker filling and fold the eggroll skin in half. Add water to the edges of the skin and fold to make them stick together. Place in boiling water for 45 seconds. Remove and sear in a hot pan with oil. Place in your favorite bowl or plate and add sauce.

Serves 4.

(Chef bio, cont'd from page 101) *and Jonathan Miller at the Stein Eriksen Lodge. During shoulder seasons when The Mustang is closed, Edgar works at Bouchon Las Vegas and to stay busy, he assists Chef Christian Ojeda at Montage Deer Valley in his spare time.*

WINE PAIRING *LOOSEN BROS., "Dr. L," Riesling, (Mosel, Germany) 2013. If there's any wine that pairs perfectly with Asian cuisine it's definitely a Riesling and this one is superb. With full flavors of peach and nectarine, Loosen Bros. really allows for your mouth to indulge in every flavor of both the dish and the wine. The off-dry in style still gives you a juicy thirst-quenching mouthful with each sip.*

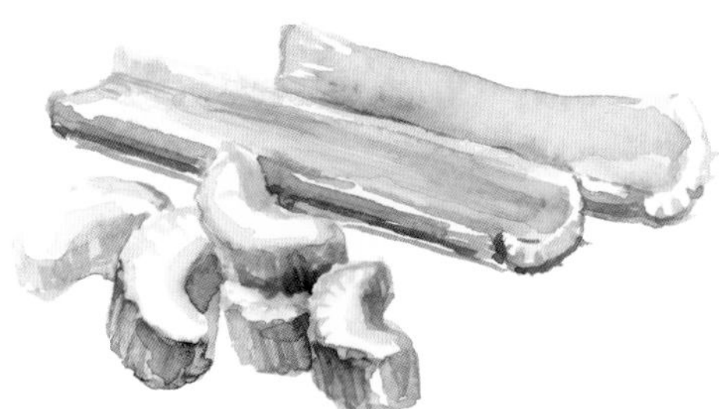

The Mustang

Lobster Bisque

MS | S

2 Maine lobsters
olive oil
½ onion, chopped
2 celery stalks, chopped

1 carrot, diced
1 cup tomato paste
2 cups heavy cream

salt & pepper to taste
chives, garnish
flour for thickening

Bring large pot of water to a boil. Add lobsters head first and boil until cooked through, about 8 minutes. Using tongs, transfer lobsters to a large bowl. Reserve 2 cups cooking liquid for later. Cool lobsters.

Working over a large bowl to catch juices, cut off lobster tails and claws. Crack tail and claw shells and remove lobster meat. Coarsely chop lobster meat, cover and chill. Coarsely chop lobster shells and bodies, transfer to medium bowl. Reserve the juices from the lobster in a large bowl.

Heat a little olive oil in a heavy large pot over high heat. Add lobster shells and bodies, and saute until shells begin to brown, about 8 minutes. Remove shells and strain into another large pot. Add onion, chopped celery stalks, diced carrot, tomato paste, and 2 cups of heavy cream. Simmer for 10 minutes and then blend ingredients together. Add a flour slurry to thicken soup to desired consistency. Add salt and pepper to taste. Use fresh lobster tail meat and chives to garnish.

Slurry

Add a tablespoon of flour to a small bowl. Add a cup of the soup slowly to thoroughly blend in the flour. When completely combined and the flour has no lumps, slowly whisk the slurry into the bisque, stirring constantly until the soup has thickened.

Serves 4.

WINE PAIRING *LOUIS JADOT, Pouilly Fuisse, (Burgundy, France) 2013. This white Burgundy will give a fantastic complement for this dish. One of the more classic Chardonnays, this wine will give the perfect balance between fruit and acidity to really allow for the dish and the wine to co-exist extremely well on the palate. With ripe flavors of peach, apple, and citrus, it will give an excellent balance of flavors. There will even be a hint of spice on the backend to accentuate the flavors of the bisque.*

SLURRY *added toward the end of cooking is an easy way to get a thicker, more luxurious sauce.*

The Mustang

Shrimp Scampi

MS | E

1 Tbsp olive oil
eight 16/20 per lb shrimp
1 Tbsp garlic, minced
1 Tbsp shallots, chopped

1 Tbsp capers
½ cup Roma tomato, diced
3 Tbsp pine nuts
½ cup white wine

½ cup butter
1 package of pasta of your choice
salt and pepper to taste

Heat olive oil in a large sauté pan over a medium heat and saueté shrimp. Once the shrimp are halfway cooked, add minced garlic, chopped shallots, capers, diced tomatoes, and pinenuts. Cook for additional 15 seconds, then add wine.

Swirl mixture to coat shrimp and sauté until liquid is reduced by half, turning shrimp to cook evenly. Add salt and pepper to taste.

After liquid is reduced, add butter. Cook pasta, according to package directions, and add to mixture.

Choosing to cook shrimp with the shell on or off is up to you. Keeping the shell on can enhance the flavor of the shrimp, although it is a bit of a challenge to take them off when mixed with the pasta sauce.

Garnish with parsley.

Serves 2

WINE PAIRING *ALOIS LAGEDER, (Trentino, Italy) 2013.*
This expressive Pinot Grigio would be a delicious pairing with the Shrimp Scampi. Qquite pronounced and lingering flowery aromas give way, as well to some spicy notes, as it truly opens up. There is a bit of rich flavor which will work well with the flavors of the dish. The finish will have a slight smokiness, but finishes very crisp and fresh.

The Mustang

Cocktail Specialties

BASILICA
1 inch slice of cucumber round
½ oz Hendrick's gin
½ oz basil simple syrup
½ lime, juiced
1 scoop ice

STRAWBERRY KEYS' LIMEADE
2-3 strawberries
1 scoop crushed ice
1½ oz Kid Curry vodka
3 oz Keys' limeade
1½ cups Nellie & Joe's Key West Lime Juice
2 cups sugar

THE MUSTANG
1¼ oz High West Rendezvous Whiskey
1 oz High West 7000 Vodka
¼ oz Domaine de Canton
Cock n'Bull ginger beer

ANNE'S PRESCRIPTION
1¼ oz of Tito's vodka
½ oz St. Germain
2 lemon wedges, juiced
Insurgent Prosecco

Basilica
Muddle cucumber in shaker. Add gin, simple syrup, lime juice and 1 scoop of ice to shaker. Shake vigorously, and double strain into martini glass. Garnish with cucumber slice and basil leaf.

Strawberry Keys' Limeade
Muddle strawberries in shaker. Add 1 scoop of ice and continue muddling until ice is crushed. Add vodka and top with Keys' Limeade. Shake and pour contents, including ice, in glass. Top with splash of soda water. Key's limeade recipe is easily made with 1½ cups Nellie & Joe's Key West Lime Juice and 2 cups of sugar cooked together to make lime syrup. To prepare limeade use half of lime syrup with water to equal 2 quarts. Garnish with lime and fresh strawberries.

The Mustang
Fill copper mug with ice. Add Rendezvous Whiskey, High West 7000 vodka and Domaine de Canton. Top with ginger beer. Garnish with lime wedge.

Anne's Prescription
Sugar the rim of champagne flute. In a shaker, add Tito's vodka, St. Germain, lemon juice and 1 scoop of ice. Shake vigorously, strain into champagne flute, and top with Prosecco. Garnish with lemon twist.

The Mustang

Key lime Cheesecake

MS | D

GRAHAM CRACKER CRUST
12 graham crackers
5 Tbsp unsalted butter, melted

FILLING
6 eggs, separated
4 lb butter, softened
1 lb cream cheese
1 cup sugar
⅔ cup key lime juice
¼ cup sugar
⅓ teaspoon salt
1 Tbsp local honey

Pre-heat oven to 350 degrees.

Graham Cracker Crust

In a food processor, pulse graham cracker crumbs, butter, sugar, salt, and honey until combined.
Firmly press mixture into a 9 inch spring form pie pan. Bake until edges are golden brown, about 12 to 15 minutes. Let cool completely.

Pie Filling

Separate the 6 eggs and set aside.
Cream the butter and cream cheese until smooth and fluffy. Add ½ cup of sugar, then add egg yolks and beat until smooth.
In another bowl, whip egg whites with remaining sugar until mixture is stiff and reaches marshmallow-like consistency. Fold into cream cheese mixture. Pour into crust-lined springform pan and bake at 350 degrees for about 45 minutes or until browned and just set. Cool and decorate with key lime slices and whipped cream .

Serves 6.

WINE PAIRING *CHATEAU STE MICHELLE Riesling (Columbia Valley, Oregon).*
A Columbia Valley Reisling is just what the Somm ordered. This off-dry Riesling will help bring out that sweet lime flavor this cheesecake has to offer. It will also enable a slight bit of peach and some slight mineral notes to be intertwined with each bite.

Myrtle
ROSE
CHOPS • COMFORT • COCKTAILS
Myrtle
ROSE
HORNITOS
STELLA ARTOIS

CHOPS • COMFORT • COCKTAILS

MYRTLE ROSE

KJ

Inspired and influenced as a young man by his Grandma Myrtle Rose, Steven Maxwell "Max", owner of Maxwell's East Coast Eatery, set out to pay homage to his late Grandmother with the creation of Myrtle Rose, Chops...Comfort...Cocktails.

Grandma Myrtle was from West Virginia and took pride in creating heartfelt comfort style dishes for her family and friends. Her recipes for chicken and biscuits, meatloaf, chicken pot pie and deliciously seared chops and steaks cooked in her famous cast iron skillet never left Max's memory of childhood dinners at Grandma's.

Wanting to pay homage to Myrtle and knowing he could fill a niche in Kimball Junction and Park City with these memorable recipes, Max created Myrtle Rose Steakhouse. The result is a well appointed space with a beautiful bar floated in the center, comfortable booths and couches, all accented with rich colors and an upbeat musical vibe. Outside, diners enjoy a beautiful mountain view, soft seating and fire accents.

And just like Grandma Myrtle, all items are made from scratch, and cast iron skillets are utilized to sear delicious chops and steaks.
Childhood recipe memories from a grandma familiar to so many of us, are now being shared for all of us to enjoy for generations to come.

OWNER/CHEF STEVEN MAXWELL

Steven "Max" Maxwell received his culinary training from Rosa Pelura, an Italian immigrant from Abruzzi, Italy. Rosa, also happens to be Max's Grandmother.

"Mom Mom" operated Pelura's Spaghetti House in Penns Grove, New Jersey in the 1930's and 40's. Along with delicious Italian fare, Rosa was an accomplished Chef, creating a "home friendly" welcoming atmosphere. Max's other grandma, Myrtle Rose, was also a talented cook and had quite the knack for creating delicious "home style" meals. Chicken pot pie, meatloaf, and delicious steaks cooked in cast iron made Myrtle quite popular with family and friends. Max had the amazing opportunity to work closely with Grandma Myrtle and pick up on the little secrets that made her food so delicious. Being part Italian, Max *(cont'd on page 112)*

CHOPS • COMFORT • COCKTAILS

Sweet Potato Hash

5 one pound sweet potatoes
1 cup apple wood smoked bacon, cooked and chopped
½ cup blended oil

3 Tbsp shallot, minced
4 cups Swiss chard, chopped
2 Tbsp, fresh garlic, minced
2 Tbsp fresh thyme, chopped

2 Tbsp fresh parsley, chopped
1 Tbsp each cracked black pepper and kosher salt
8 oz goat cheese, crumbled

Preheat oven to 375 degrees.

Wash sweet potatoes and place on a baking sheet. Place in oven and roast 45 minutes. Potatoes should still be firm when removed from oven. Allow potatoes to cool slightly and remove skins. Place on cutting board and cut into medium size cubes.

In stovetop pan, cook the smoked bacon thoroughly. Remove from stove, drain, chop and set aside for later.

Place a large cast iron skillet on medium low heat. Pour blended oil into pan and allow to heat. Add in the minced shallots and sauté until slightly brown. Add the sweet potato cubes and the chopped Swiss chard. Stir gently every 3-5 minutes. As the chard begins to wilt, add in the garlic, thyme, parsley, salt and pepper. Finally, add in the bacon and goat cheese. Stir gently. Add additional salt and pepper to taste. Serve immediately.

10 Servings

(Chef Maxwell bio, cont'd from page 111) was born with the gift of being naturally hospitable and has made a name for himself from New Jersey to Florida and out to Utah. Max's excellent palette combined with sincere hospitality, has proven to be the perfect recipe combination.

CHOPS • COMFORT • COCKTAILS

Roasted Autumn Brussels Sprouts

3 lbs fresh Brussels sprouts
¼ cup blended oil
1 Tbsp cracked black pepper
1 Tbsp kosher salt

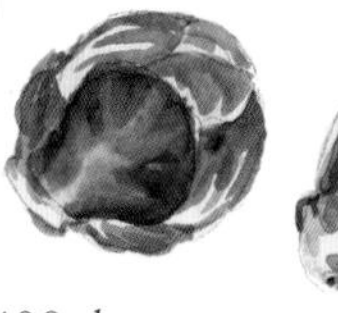

COMPOTE
1 cup golden raisins
1 cup dark raisins
1 cup pitted prunes
2 cups brown sugar
2 cups apple juice
3 Tbsp balsamic vinegar
1 Tbsp cracked black pepper
1 Tbsp kosher salt

GARNISH
1 cup pistachios

Preheat oven to 400 degrees.

Trim sprouts and cut in half thru the core. Place in medium size bowl and toss with oil, salt and pepper, and set aside.

Compote

In a medium size sauce pot combine the golden raisins, dark raisins, pitted prunes, brown sugar, apple juice, balsamic vinegar, cracked black pepper and kosher salt.

On low heat, simmer until the fruit is extremely soft, approximately 90 minutes. If liquid evaporates before fruit is tender, add in 1 cup of water and continue to simmer. Place compote in a food processor and pulse to a slightly chunky consistency. Transfer to a small bowl and place uncovered in refrigerator.

Brussels Sprouts

Place Brussels sprouts on a baking sheet and roast in oven 45-50 minutes until they begin to slightly brown. Remove from oven and place in a medium bowl. Add in ½ cup of the prepared compote and ¼ cup pistachios and mix well. Place in a serving bowl and garnish with remainder of pistachios and enjoy immediately.

Note

Remaining compote can be stored covered in the refrigerator for up to one week and used as a garnish for a grilled Pork Chop or Tenderloin, or as an accompaniment to your favorite cheeses.

Myrtle's Meat Loaf with French Whipped Potatoes

MEAT LOAF
10 oz coarsely ground veal
10 oz ground meat blend
10 oz ground pork
12 oz chili sauce
1 carrot, peeled and minced
¼ Spanish onion, finely diced
2 cloves of garlic, minced
¼ red pepper, finely diced
½ cup of breadcrumbs
2 eggs, beaten
2 Tbsp of Worcestershire sauce
2 Tbsp of Dijon mustard
10 slices of uncooked maple bacon
2 tsp cumin seeds
2 tsp fennel seeds
¾ cup cold water
½ cup olive oil
salt and pepper to taste

MASHED POTATOES
2 lbs Yukon Gold potatoes, unpeeled
2 cups whole milk
1 lb unsalted butter, diced and
kept well chilled until ready to use
kosher salt to taste
white pepper to taste

Preheat oven to 350 degrees.

In large bowl, mix together coarsely ground veal, ground meat blend, ground pork, chili sauce, minced carrots, finely diced spanish onion, minced garlic, finely diced red pepper, breadcrumbs, well beaten eggs, Worcestershire sauce, Dijon mustard, cumin seeds, fennel seeds, cold water, olive oil and salt and pepper to taste.

Divide mixture into 6 oz portions. Wrap with raw bacon and place in mini tins. Bake at 350 degrees for 1 hour. Top with your favorite meatloaf sauce or gravy.

Mashed Potatoes

Place the potatoes in a saucepan with 2 quarts cold water and one tablespoon coarse salt. Bring to a simmer, cover, and cook until a knife slips in and out of the potatoes easily and cleanly, about 25 minutes.

Drain the potatoes and peel them. Put them through a potato ricer (or a food mill fitted with its finest disk) into a large saucepan. Turn the heat under the saucepan to medium and dry the potato flesh slightly by turning it vigorously with a spatula for about 5 minutes.

In the meantime, rinse a small saucepan, pour out the excess water, but do not wipe it dry. Add the milk and bring to a boil. Turn the heat under the potatoes to low and incorporate the well-chilled butter bit by bit, stirring it in energetically for a smooth, creamy finish. Pour in the hot milk in a thin ring, stiring until all the milk has been absorbed. Turn off the heat. Add salt and pepper to taste.

Serves 8

WINE PAIRING *CONNCREEK Cab Franc (Napa Valley, California) 2013. The Conn Creek vineyard is a very small boutique winery right on the Silverado Trail in the Rutherford district. Rutherford is located just above Oakville and below St. Helena. This wine has a perfect balance of raspberry and cocoa. This, however, opens up to a fantastic bouquet of cedar and a slight hint of mocha. The raspberry and cocoa continues through to the finish with a slight balance of toasted spice as well.*

Maryland Style Crab Cakes with Remoulade Sauce

- 1 cup mayo, preferably Hellmann's
- 2 eggs
- 1 Tbsp Dijon mustard
- 3 tsp Worcestershire Sauce
- 1 Tbsp Old Bay Seasoning
- 3 Tbsp crushed Ritz crackers
- 1 Tbsp chopped parsley
- 1 lb lump crabmeat

REMOULADE SAUCE

- 2 cups mayonnaise, preferably Hellmann's
- ½ cup finely chopped scallions, green parts only
- 2 Tbsp finely chopped fresh flat-leaf parsley
- 2 Tbsp minced capers
- 2 Tbsp finely chopped celery
- 2 Tbsp Creole, or other whole-grain mustard
- 1½ tsp minced garlic
- 3 tsp sweet paprika
- 1 tsp hot sauce, such as Crystal
- ½ tsp salt
- ¼ tsp freshly ground black pepper

Preheat oven to 400 degrees.

Crab Cakes

In a small mixing bowl combine mayo, Dijon mustard, Worcestershire sauce, Old Bay Seasoning, crushed Ritz crackers, and chopped parsley and mix well.

Place crabmeat into a separate bowl and fold half of cracker mixture into crabmeat. If necessary, add a bit more mix so that crabmeat is formable, but not overly wet.
Scoop into balls and press gently, onto cookie sheet. Do not smash. Bake in oven for approximately 15 minutes until golden brown.

Remoulade Sauce

In a small mixing bowl, combine Hellmann's mayonnaise, finely chopped scallions, finely chopped fresh flat-leaf parsley, minced capers, finely chopped celery, Creole, or other whole-grain mustard, minced garlic, sweet paprika, hot sauce, salt, and freshly ground black pepper. Adjust to preferred taste. Can be refrigerated, covered, up to one week.

Serves 4

WINE PAIRING *MARCEL DEISS Reisling (Alsace, France) 2015. From Northeastern France in the Alsace region, Marcel Deiss's Reisling will pair deliciously with the crab cakes. Since there is a little bit of spice with the Old Bay and the Worcestershire Sauce, a little bit of sweetness swill complement the dish. The nose of white fruit and citrus zests gives way to a delicious flavor of lemon, pineapple, and a bit of white peach. This should give your taste buds a slight break from the heat of the crab cake.*

Herb Butter for Steaks & Chops

1 lb butter
3 Tbsp chopped parsley
2 Tbsp roasted garlic
3 Tbsp cracked black pepper
1 Tbsp salt

Place butter in a mixing bowl and allow to soften, approximately 30 minutes. Add remaining ingredients and blend until well incorporated.

Place butter mix onto a sheet of parchment paper and roll into a log. Refrigerate for up to 4 days. To serve, slice off wheels of butter and place under your steaks or chops after you take them off the grill and before placing on a serving platter.

Four Tips for a Perfectly cooked Steak

One

Salt and pepper your steak well before cooking for the deepest seasoning and best browning. Try seasoning your steak with kosher salt and cracked black pepper.

Two

When it's time to cook, high heat is key to ensure an even deep brown crust. It's also best to use a cast-iron skillet or other heavy-duty pan that will retain heat once the steak hits the pan. Brush the skillet lightly with vegetable oil and heat it on the stove until wisps of smoke rise from the surface. Then place the steak in the center and sear it well on the top, bottom, and edges. Then finish cooking your steaks or chops in a 400 degree oven.

Three

There are many ways to guesstimate doneness, but the most reliable way is with a meat thermometer. Shoot for medium rare or 135 degree reading.

Four

Before you serve your steak, allow it to rest for 5 to 10 minutes. This will allow the juices to redistribute for a more luscious steak. Then, try topping your steak with this delicious compound butter recipe.

WINE PAIRING *CHATEAU LYONNAT Left Bank Blend (Bordeaux, France) 2009.*
A delicious right bank Bordeaux that is amazing with Steaks and Chops. All Bordeaux on the right bank are Merlot driven and left bank are Cabernet Sauvignon. This wine gives an amazing deep garnet color with a nose of spiced bread and red fruits such as ripe plum and black cherry. The finish is a slight hint of coffee and vanilla.

POWDER

POWDER

POWDER AT WALDORF ASTORIA

CV

Established in December of 2011 and led by Executive Chef Ryker Brown, Powder restaurant at Waldorf Astoria Park City is located at the heart of Canyons Village base of Park City Resort. Chef Ryker is encouraged by the bountiful mountains of Utah to create brilliant menu offerings that are inspired by local farmers.

Treat yourself to a mouth-watering seasonal menu inspired by the finest local ingredients with unique, fresh and flavorful offerings for the entire family. Here, technique and imagination are balanced with fresh cuisine and the heartiness of the mountains to create an exceptional, flavor-focused dining experience.

Powder takes pride in sourcing as many local ingredients as possible and letting the flavor of the food shine through in creative dishes such as the signature Fried Organic Chicken. The cuisine focus is on direct, unique flavor with modern presentation. The dishes and cocktails at Powder even pull honey from their on-property bee 'sanctuary' (as they like to call the hive) that hosts over 70,000 bees, or from Chef Ryker's roof top garden that provides herbs for his dishes throughout the seasons.

Powder is open for breakfast, lunch, après-ski and dinner daily to encourage you to treat yourself to a seasonal modern mountain menu, driven by the seasons and inspired by the finest local ingredients. The restaurant also offers an unparalleled wine and spirits program. In 2016, Powder introduced their very own custom rye pale ale from Park City Brewery, which is appropriately named Pow Day. Short for Powder Day, a "Pow Day" is referred to as the best kind of ski day on the mountain—where mountain riders are engulfed in Utah's light and fluffy snow while cruising through acres of trails.

Bonus Bark City Dog treats from Powders bark series.

EXECUTIVE CHEF RYKER BROWN

While his culinary career began in California, Brown has spent most of his career working in mountain resort destinations including Big Sky Resort and the Yellowstone Club at Rainbow Lodge as Executive Sous Chef at each.

In 2008, he accepted the Executive Chef position at Promontory Ranch Club, and worked his way to Sundance Mountain Resort as the Resort Executive Chef from 2012-2014.

Ryker combines traditional techniques with new methods, such as sous-vide and basted meats. His focus on natural ingredients has enhanced Powder's use of local products, including Heber Valley Cheese, Creminelli cured meats for charcuteries, and the use of herbs and honey from Waldorf Astoria Park City's backyard garden and beehive.

POWDER

Seared Diver Scallops with Garlic Puree and Meyer Lemon Preserve

MEYER LEMON PRESERVE
(preserve is a 3 month process)
1 lb Meyer lemon, washed and quartered
2 cups kosher salt
2 cups granulated sugar
6 sprigs fresh thyme
20 black peppercorns
2 bay leaves
2 cups lemon Juice
2 Tbsp champagne vinegar
1 Tbsp olive oil
1 lemon, juice

GARLIC PUREE
1 cup garlic cloves, peeled
1 Tbsp heavy cream

1 Tbsp canola oil
2-3 divers scallops per portion
2 Tbsp butter

GARNISH
¼ cup fresh English peas or sugar snap peas
6 asparagus, trimmed and sliced
1 tsp garlic, chopped
1 Tbsp butter

Meyer Lemon Preserve

Mix quartered lemon, kosher salt, sugar, thyme, black peppercorns, bay leaves, and lemon juice together and place in a plastic container, making sure liquid is almost covering lemons. Cover and place in a cooler for 3-5 months. Remove from container and rinse with cold water. Remove inside of lemons leaving only the outside rind. Dice lemon rind, which is now very soft, and mix with champagne vinegar, olive oil and the juice of one lemon.

Garlic Puree

In a medium size stock pot, bring water to boil. Add garlic and cook for 3-5 minutes. Remove from heat and shock in a bowl of ice water. Remove from ice and return to boiling water. Repeat the steps 15 times until the garlic is very soft. After blanching is complete, remove garlic from boiling water and add to blender. Add heavy cream and season with salt and pepper. Puree on high until mixture is smooth.

Scallops

(It's important to note that the scallops should be very dry. Before cooking, lay them on a clean paper towel and pat dry.)
Heat 10 inch sauté pan over high heat and add 1 Tbsp canola oil. Season scallops and sear in a pan.
Cook for approximately 1-2 minutes or until scallops have reached a deep golden brown. Flip each scallop over and remove from heat. Add butter to the pan and baste for 2 minutes. Let rest.

Assembly

Heat saute pan with 1 Tbsp vegetable oil. Add peas and asparagus and cook for 1-2 minutes. Add garlic and butter. Season with salt and pepper.
Assemble all components on plate. Garnish with any type of greens. We use pea tendrils, tat soi leaves or watercress.

POWDER

Kurobuta Pork Belly, Pickled Ramps, Mustard and Peas

2 lbs raw whole pork belly

CURE MIXTURE
1 cup kosher salt
1 Tbsp fennel seeds, ground
1 Tbsp mustard seeds, ground
1 Tbsp coriander seeds, ground
¼ cup granulated sugar
½ gallon chicken stock

PICKLED RAMPS
3 cup rice wine vinegar
1 tsp fennel seeds
1 tsp mustard seeds
3 gloves garlic, peeled
1 Tbsp granulated sugar
8 oz fresh ramps, washed (if you can't find ramps, green scallions would be a great replacement)

PEA PUREE
2 cups fresh English peas
2 Tbsp cold butter
½ cup heavy cream
salt and pepper

PICKLED MUSTARD SEEDS
2 cups mustard seeds
3 cups white balsamic vinegar
2 Tbsp granulated sugar

Preheat oven to 275 degrees.

For the cure mixture, combine salt, fennel, mustard, coriander and sugar in a mixing bowl. Sprinkle both sides of pork belly and lay on sheet pan. Wrap in plastic wrap and place in the refrigerator for 12 hours or overnight. Remove from cooler and rinse with cold water. Dry with paper towels and place in a braising pan. Add chicken stock then cover with plastic wrap and a top layer of aluminum foil.

Place pork in the oven for 8-10 hours or until pork belly is very tender. Remove from oven and allow to cool for 30 minutes. Remove pork from pan and place on a sheet pan. Move to cooler and allow to cool for at least 8 hours. Cut into long strips, about 5 ounces each. To complete, heat 10 inch sauté pan on high with 1 Tbsp vegetable oil. Season pork belly slices and pan sear till crispy golden brown on each side.

Pickled Ramps

In a medium saucepan, add rice wine vinegar, fennel, mustard, garlic, and sugar and bring to a boil. Add ramps and remove from heat. Let cool in the liquid for up to 7 days.

Pea Puree

Bring a small pot of salted water to a boil. Add peas and cook for 1 minute. Remove peas from water and add to blender. Add butter and cream and puree on high until smooth. If mixture is too thick, use the blanching water to thin. Season with salt and pepper.

Pickled Mustard Seeds

Heat a small sauce pan with water and boil. Blanch mustard seeds for 1 minute and drain. Rinse under cold water and transfer to a small container.

Boil vinegar and sugar and add to mustard seeds. Allow to cool at room temperature and cover.

Serves 8.

POWDER

Fried Organic Chicken with "Mac-n-Cheese", Broccolini, Jalapeno, Bacon, Fennel, Chicken Gravy

Cryovac vacuum bags
immersion circulator
four 10 oz organic boneless chicken breasts, skin on
2 cups plus 4 Tbsp buttermilk
8 fresh thyme sprigs
3 cups seasoned flour
8 cups canola oil for frying

SEASONED FLOUR
2 cups all-purpose flour
1 tsp dried thyme
2 Tbsp paprika
½ tsp cayenne pepper
2 Tbsp kosher salt
1 Tbsp granulated garlic
1 Tbsp onion powder
1 tsp cumin
2 Tbsp chili powder

MAC-N-CHEESE
2 cups orzo pasta, al dente
¾ cups heavy cream
1 Tbsp mascarpone cheese
½ cups gruyere cheese, grated
salt & pepper
1 Tbsp fresh herb mixture, chopped (Italian parsley, tarragon, chives and dill)

CHICKEN GRAVY
5 lbs chicken bones, roasted
¼ cup canola oil
2 onions, peeled and chopped
10 cloves garlic, peeled, whole
2 carrots, peeled and chopped
3 celery stalks, chopped
3 Tbsp tomato paste
1 cup red wine
10 sprigs fresh thyme
1 tsp black peppercorn

FINISHING
1 tsp canola oil
½ lb brocollini, trimmed
½ cups leeks, washed, chopped, blanched
1 tsp garlic, chopped
1 Tbsp white wine
1 Tbsp butter, cubed
salt and pepper
1 cups bacon, chopped and rendered until crispy
1 fennel bulb, shaved thinly on mandolin
dill leaves
sliced jalapeno
½ cup pickles, sliced (we make our own, but use your favorite brand)

In individual plastic Cryovac bags, place a raw chicken breast, 1 Tbsp of buttermilk and lay 2 sprigs of thyme on each chicken breast. On highest pressure, seal each bag in a chamber vacuum sealer.

Fill heavy-duty plastic container with water and turn on Immersion Circulator to 155 degrees. Place chicken in circulator for 55 minutes. Remove from water and allow to rest for 5-10 minutes. In the meantime, heat oil in a heavy duty sauce pan until the temperature reaches 355 degrees.

For Seasoned Flour

In a separate mixing bowl, mix all-purpose flour, dried thyme, paprika, cayenne pepper, kosher salt, granulated garlic, onion powder, cumin and chili powder together in a mixing bowl. Place the remaining 3 Tbsp buttermilk in a separate mixing bowl.

Cut chicken into three pieces and dredge in flour, then dip into buttermilk, remove and return to flour. Allow 5 minutes for the flour to adhere to the chicken. Place coated chicken in a pan with hot oil and deep fry until crispy golden color, approximately 3 minutes. Remove chicken from oil and place onto a paper towel lined pan. Season with salt.

Mac-n-Cheese

In a medium saucepan, add water and salt and bring to a boil. Add pasta and boil. Taste pasta to check tenderness. Remove from stove and drain the pasta. In saucepan *(Cont'd on page 125)*

POWDER

Fried Organic Chicken with "Mac-n-Cheese", Broccolini, Jalapeno, Bacon, Fennel, Chicken Gravy *(cont'd)*

(Fried Chicken, cont'd from page 124) heat heavy cream to boil. Add cooked pasta and continue to simmer. Add cheeses and herbs and cook until mixture reaches a creamy consistency. Season to taste.

Chicken Gravy

Roast the 5 lbs of chicken bones in a 450 degree oven for 3 hours or until bones reach a dark brown color.

In a large stock pot, place chicken bones and add enough water until it just covers the bones. Let simmer for 18 hours. Remove bones from water, strain liquid into a container, and reserve. Should yield approximately 8-10 cups.

In a large roasting pan, heat oil and add onions and garlic. Cook until nicely caramelized. Add carrots and celery. Continue to cook until dark brown, but not burnt. Add tomato paste and cook for another 5 minutes. Add red wine, thyme and peppercorn. Allow alcohol to burn off (1 minute) and then add chicken stock. Simmer for 2-3 hours or until it reaches a maple syrup consistency. Strain several times through a fine strainer.

Finish

In a medium sauté pan, heat canola oil. Add brocollini, leeks and garlic. Season. Cook until the color starts to stand out. Add white wine, and butter and check seasoning again.

Assembly

Place a long strip of mac-n-cheese on one side of plate. (Mac-n-cheese should hold together and not be loose). Place broccolini and leeks on top of pasta. Arrange bacon around vegetables. Place chicken on top of all. Garnish with shaved fennel, dill leaves, jalapeno and sliced pickles. Serve chicken gravy on the side.

Serves 4-6

BEER PAIRING *PARK CITY BREWERY'S Pow Day after the best kind of day on the mountain. A rye pale ale brewed to pair with Chef Ryker's signature dishes.Park City's Rye Pale Ale, also known as the Pow Day Rye Pale Ale at Waldorf Astoria Hotels, is a unique twist on both an American and English pale ale. Making use of English caramel malts to provide a sweet malt back bone and northwest American hops for bittering and floral flavor and citrus aroma, Park City's Rye Pale Ale provides balance and delicate complexity. And the addition of rye offers a dry, slightly peppery, spicy, yet clean finish.*

— Brian Ray, Park City Brewery

IMMERSION CIRCULATOR *is for sous vide food cooking, and uses sealed packages in a prolonged water bath at lower temperatures than usually cooked.*

POWDER

Grilled Heirloom Carrots with Thai Curried Yogurt

6 each baby heirloom carrots, peeled and blanched
2 Tbsp olive oil

salt and pepper to taste
6 basil leaves, chiffonade
2 tsp butter
¼ cup plain Greek yogurt

1 Tbsp red curry paste
1 lime, juice only
½ head cauliflower
salt and pepper to taste

Preheat grill on high.

Cut carrots in half and toss in oil. Season with salt and pepper and place on hot grill. Grill until slightly charred. Remove from heat and toss with basil and 1 tsp butter. Set aside.

In a mixing bowl, blend yogurt, curry paste and lime juice. Smear on plate.

In a food processor, add cauliflower florets and grind until cauliflower resembles couscous.
Heat sauté pan and add cauliflower to pan. Add remaining 1 tsp of butter and season with salt and pepper.

Assembly

Place carrots over yogurt. Sprinkle cauliflower over carrots and garnish with carrot tops.

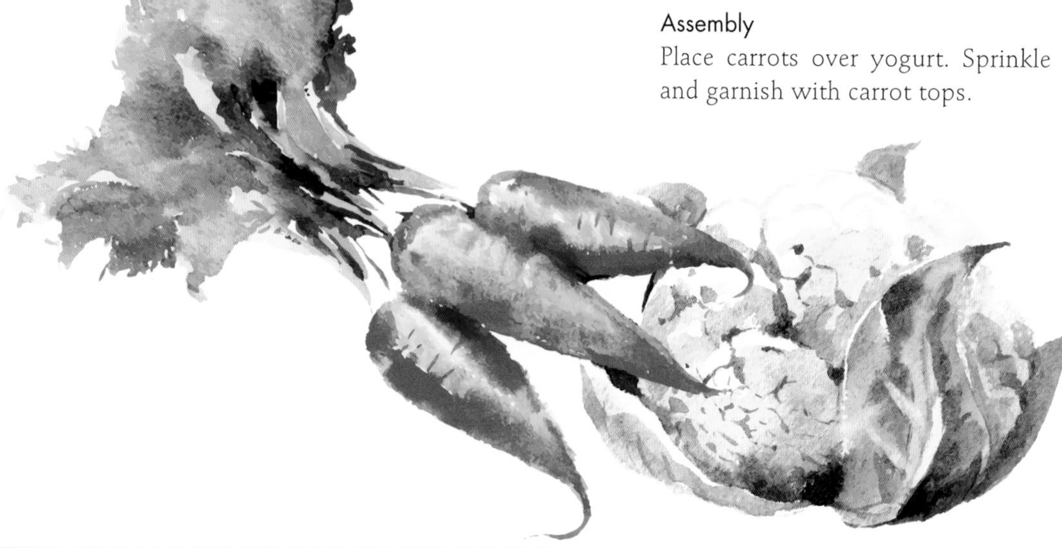

CHIFFONADE is a method of chopping herbs and leafy green vegetables such as basil and spinach. For this recipe, stack the basil leaves together and then cut perpendicular to the roll. The end result will be long thin strips of your greens.

POWDER

Waldorf Astoria Beignets

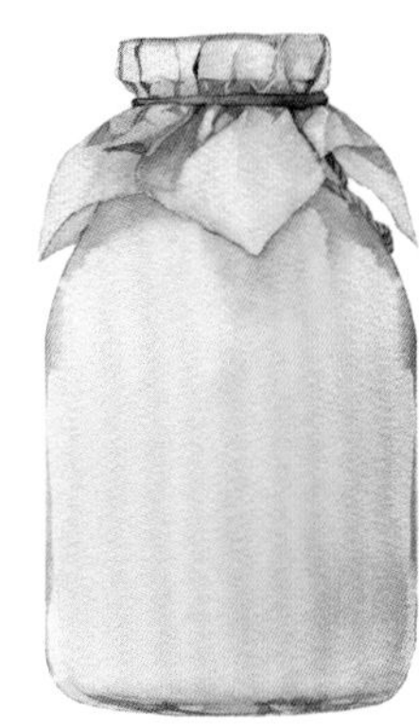

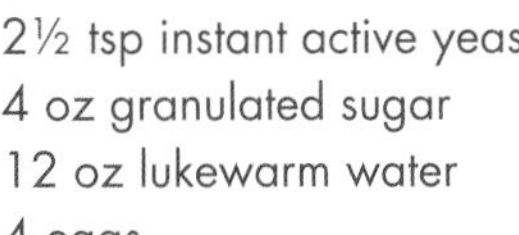

2½ tsp instant active yeast
4 oz granulated sugar
12 oz lukewarm water
4 eggs
8 oz evaporated milk
1 tsp salt
3 lbs high gluten bread flour
2 oz vegetable shortening

In a small bowl mix the yeast, granulated sugar and lukewarm water in a bowl and allow the yeast to activate for ten minutes.

In a separate bowl, mix together the eggs, evaporated milk and salt. In a mixing bowl, measure out the high gluten flour and shortening. When the yeast is activated, add it to the egg and evaporated milk mixture.

Using a dough hook, turn the mixer on and add the wet ingredients to the flour shortening mixture and mix until the dough comes together.

Take the dough out of the bowl and put it in a bowl large enough for the dough to double in size.
Let dough rise in a warm spot for two hours.
Once dough has doubled in size, roll the dough out on a floured surface to a ½ inch thickness.
Cut into desired shapes and fry in oil at 350 degrees.

Assembly
Sprinkle with powdered sugar.
Serve with vanilla creme anglaise or light dessert custard and raspberry coulis.

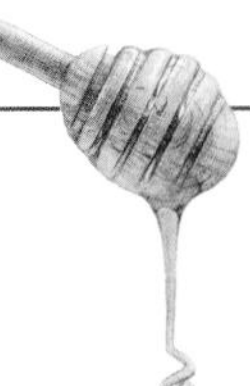

Waldorf Astoria "Bark" City Dog Treats

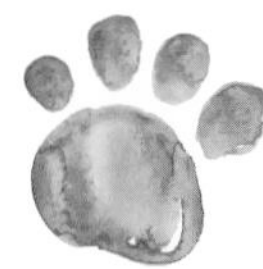

1 cup flour
1 banana
3 oz peanut butter
2 oz milk
1 Tbsp honey
⅓ cup oats

Preheat oven to 350 degrees.
Place flour, banana, peanut butter, milk, honey and oats in a bowl and mix together by hand until combined.
Flour table or cutting board to keep mixture from sticking.
Place dough on table and roll out to desired thickness.
Cut your fun shapes or stamp with a dog biscuit shaped cutter.
Bake for 8 minutes, flip treats over and bake another 5 minutes.

AUGUST 12-14
arts festival
UnitedHealthcare
KÜHL
UTAH
SUBARU
KÜHL

REDROCK
BREWERY

RED ROCK BREWERY

KJ

Red Rock Brewery opened its doors on March 14, 1994. From the very beginning, we set out to brew high-quality craft beers and serve delicious food.

In the past 20 years, Red Rock Brewery has earned a national reputation as one of the most creative breweries in the country. Our beers have earned more than 100 regional and national awards and our restaurant has been named "Brew Pub of the Year" by Brewpub Magazine and "Large Brewpub of the Year" by the Great American Beer Festival.

Locally, the original brew pub has become a staple of Salt Lake City's downtown dining scene, and the company opened additional locations in Kimball Junction (near the resort community of Park City) and in Fashion Place (located in the middle of the Salt Lake Valley).

In 2011, Red Rock expanded our brewing capacity with a dedicated brewery to support our restaurant growth and expand the availability of our beers to local pubs and retail locations. Now we produce six brands of high point beer that can be purchased from the Utah State Liquor stores, our restaurants and many other locations throughout Utah and the United States.

Throughout our development, Red Rock Brewery has remained true to its goals of high-quality craft beers and delicious food. We welcome you to our community.

BREWERY

At Red Rock Brewery, with our craft original and unique new beers, we look for inspiration anywhere and everywhere, leading to creative brews like our award winning Red Rock Rêve, the barrel aged Belgian-style tripple ale; the dandelion-based Paardebloem; and Secale, a Bavarian-style doppelbock lager created with High West Distillery and aged in their rye whiskey barrels for six months.

Our Draft Classic beers fall into a "Session" category. A typical session beer contains less than 5% ABV, is well balanced and very drinkable.

Fine Line beers are bigger and bolder than our Draft Classics and are brewed with passion and patience.

Artist Palette expresses variety & creativity in beer making. It's an opportunity for our brewers to hone their craft and expand the possibilities of what beer can be.

Mexican Steamed Mussels

1 corn on the cob, steamed and grilled
1 cup white wine
½ cup chipotle butter
1 jalapeño, sliced in super thin rings
1 poblano pepper, diced
1 cup tomato, diced
1 small shallot, diced
12 to 15 mussels per guest

Mussels

In a large pot, add enough water to steam the corn. Then place the corn on the grill. When done, slice the corn off the cob.
In a large sauté pan, add the wine and butter and heat over medium heat until butter is melted. When butter is melted, add the corn, sliced Jalapeño peppers, diced pablano peppers, diced tomatoes, and diced shallots and to the pan.
Simmer mixture for 5 minutes. Stir well while adding a splash more wine. Then add the mussels.
Cover and allow for mussels to fully open. Discard unopened shells.
Add the chipotle butter slowly to reach the desired spiciness.
Portion out mussels then pour broth over top.

Chipotle Butter

Whip butter slowly adding chipotle peppers until you reach desired spiciness.

Notes

Since adding a daily Chef's creation of steamed mussels, this recipe has become a favorite of our regulars. Oftentimes they request this preparation even if it isn't on the daily board. Be sure to have some bread to soak up this delicious broth.

BEER PAIRING *Landon Olsen, Certified Cicerone® recommends. Le Quatre Saison 6.2% alcohol by volume. The Mexican-style ingredients and mild heat of this dish will pair wonderfully with the initial citrus bite of our Le Quatre Saison. This farmhouse-style brew has a fruity and spicy character from the expressive yeast strain and a slight grainy malt flavor that will play delightfully well with the vegetal flavors of pepper and corn. It will also provide a bone-dry and highly carbonated finish that will scrub the tongue clean and get you ready for the next bite.*

Peach and Caramelized Onion Soup

2 large yellow onions, julienned
8 oz butter
1 cup brown sugar
1 cup white wine
2½ lbs peaches, peeled, pitted and sliced

8 oz lemon juice
1 Tbsp ground cinnamon
1 Tbsp ground nutmeg
16 cups vegetable stock
2 cups heavy cream
1½ lb cream cheese

CRÉME FRAICHE
1 cup heavy cream
2 Tbsp buttermilk

Créme Fraiche

Combine heavy cream and buttermilk in a glass bowl. Stir well and cover with a warm kitchen towel.
Store mixture at room temperature (about 70°F) overnight or until very thick.

Caramelized Onions

Peel, quarter and julienne onions. Then caramelize onions by slowly cooking them in butter and brown sugar until browned. Remove the onions from the pot and reserve until later.

Peach Soup

Deglaze pot with 1 cup of white wine and reduce the wine to half.
Add peaches to wine reduction and brown until golden and translucent. Add lemon juice, cinnamon, nutmeg, vegetable stock, heavy cream and cream cheese. Bring to a boil and simmer for 20 minutes until soup is thick.
Puree soup until smooth.

Assembly

Add caramelized onions to the soup, and season with salt and pepper to taste.
Garnish with fresh mint and créme fraiche.

BEER PAIRING *Landon Olsen, Certified Cicerone® recommends. Griswald's Holiday Ale 8.5% alcohol by volume. Although we only release this beer once a year, I couldn't help but think it'd be the perfect pairing. Our Griswald's Holiday Ale is brewed with nutmeg, coriander, orange peel, and cinnamon and would be a perfect pairing for this sweet, savory, and creamy soup that has its own hint of spice. The spice complements the peach, while the alcoholic warmth and caramel malt flavor of the beer would provide a well balanced finish to the onions and overall creamy nature of the soup.*

Warm Shrimp Salad

2 large sweet potatoes
2 large grapefruits
1 large bunch spinach
1 large bunch watercress
½ lb of 26/30 shrimp
2 Tbsp butter
½ cup white wine

CREAMY LEMON PEPPER DRESSING
1 cup low fat mayonnaise
1 cup buttermilk
1½ Tbsp honey
1½ Tbsp fresh lime juice
¼ tsp cracked black pepper
1 Tbsp white wine vinegar
½ tsp chopped parsley
2 Tbsp water

Garnish
1 cup gorgonzola cheese
½ cup pistachios, toasted

Preheat oven to 350 degrees.

Creamy Lemon Pepper Dressing

Whisk together low fat mayo, buttermilk, honey, Roses lime juice, cracked black pepper, white wine vinegar, parsley and water until blended.

Salad

Roast sweet potatoes. Peel the potatoes and cut lengthwise into 8 slices per potato. Keep warm. Remove grapefruit skins and section. Wash, cut and toss spinach and watercress. Peel and clean shrimp, then sauté with white wine and butter.

Assembly

Toss salad greens in dressing and plate. Place an equal portion sweet potatoes, grapefruit, cheese, and pistachios on each then add shrimp.

Server 4 guests.

Notes

This salad is a classic, enjoyed by our regulars since our doors opened. Amazing flavors and a generous size portion can make it an entrée to be enjoyed by friends on a summer night.

BEER PAIRING *Landon Olsen, Certified Cicerone® recommends. Golden Halo Blonde Ale 5.8%. Alcohol by volume. Our Golden Halo Blonde Ale is a delightfully light and balanced beer with a spicy, floral aroma and a subdued malty sweetness that will complement the Warm Shrimp Salad perfectly… without overpowering it. The creamy lemon pepper dressing, watercress and spinach will pair wonderfully with the earthy spice of the Noble Hops, while the sweetness of the roasted sweet potato will match well with the beer's sweet malty finish and provide a contrast with the tart citrus of the grapefruit.*

French Onion Steak Sandwich

- 2 large yellow onions, peeled, quartered, julienned
- 4 oz butter
- 2 Tbsp brown sugar
- 4 8 oz NY strip steaks
- 1 sourdough baguette
- 1 cup shredded Gruyere
- 1 cup shredded Mozzarella cheese

FRENCH ONION SOUP

- 2 oz butter
- 3 mid size yellow onions, sliced long
- 1 ¼ cups of Sauterne wine
- 1 ¼ cups of Burgundy wine
- ½ cup of beef base
- 4 cups chicken stock
- 2 bay leaves
- 4 cups of water

In a large sauté pan, add butter and onions and sauté until browned. Add both, the Sauterne and Burgundy wines and reduce by half. Add the beef base, chicken stock, bay leaves, and water, and simmer for 45 minutes.

Grill steak to desired temperature. Allow steaks to rest at room temperature.

Caramelized Onions

Peel, quarter and jullienne onions. Then caramelize onions by slowly cooking them in butter and brown sugar.

Assembly

Slice the baguette into ½ inch pieces so you have 16 slices. Rub with olive oil and toast lightly. Grill steaks to desired temperature. Allow to rest slightly then cut short side to fan out. Top baguette with cheese and melt. Lay out two pieces of toast per plate, lay steaks across and smother with caramelized onions. Top with melted cheese baguette.

Serves 4.

Notes

This Red Rock classic offers two recipes in one. By creating one of our iconic sandwich dishes, which guest will need a knife and fork to eat, you will also be able to serve our French onion soup that has warmed bellys for years.

BEER PAIRING *Landon Olsen, Certified Cicerone® recommends. Bobcat Nutbrown Ale 6.1% alcohol by volume. An easy choice! The caramelized onions, grilled steak, gruyere and mozzarella cheeses perfectly complement our Bobcat Nutbrown Ale. The dank northwest hops complement the caramelized onions and au jus, while the chocolate and crystal malts pair ideally with the grilled steak, gruyere and mozzarella cheese. The carbonation of the beer scrubs the palette clean after every rich and delicious bite of this popular dish.*

RedRock Brewery

Frosted Carrot Cake

CAKE
4 cups all purpose flour
1 ¼ cups sugar
1 Tbsp baking soda
2 tsp cinnamon
4 eggs
1 ⅜ cups vegetable oil
1 ½ lbs shredded carrots

FROSTING
½ lb butter
½ lb cream cheese
1 ½ lb powdered sugar
¼ oz fresh lemon juice
2 tsp vanilla
½ orange, juiced

Preheat oven to 350 degrees.

Carrot Cake

Grease 9 x12 baking dish.
Mix dry ingredients; flour, sugar, baking soda, cinnamon together. Slowly fold in eggs and oil.
Add carrots and combine thoroughly.
Bake at 350 degrees for 85 minutes. Cool before cutting.

Frosting

Cream the butter and cream cheese until smooth. Slowly blend in the powdered sugar, then add the lemon juice, vanilla, and orange juice. Mix well for a smooth creamy consistency. Allow to chill for half hour. When cake is completely cooled, spread generously over carrot cake.

Servers 4-6

Notes

Some desserts come and go with the seasons. Some lose a following over time and are taken off a menu. Our carrot cake is neither of those. Super moist, loaded with shredded carrots, and frosted with a cream cheese frosting that customers always want more of, this dessert is what your guests will crave for a final course. An easy recipe that doesn't need a degree in baking to create and impress, leftovers are enjoyed for days.

BEER PAIRING *Landon Olsen, Certified Cicerone® recommends: Elephino Double IPA 8% alcohol by volume. The key with pairing beer and this popular dessert is balance. Elephino Double IPA is snappy and bitter with a lot of citrus and floral attributes that come from the addition of lively American hops. When paired with our super sweet and tangy Carrot Cake, the bitterness and sweetness of this match made in heaven contrast one another by performing the perfect balancing act.*

SHABU
FREESTYLE ASIAN CUISINE

SHABU

Shabu Shabu is a Japanese "hot pot" meal that lets you customize your meal with a selection of savory broths, made-to-order Bento boxes and a variety of dipping sauces. When your Bento Box is empty, fresh Udon noodles are ladled into the flavored broth to create a rich and simple soup. Shabu Shabu traces back to 13th Century Mongolia during the rule of Genghis Khan. Nomadic armies developed this "hot pot" cooking method as a way to stay nourished and conserve fuel supplies while on the move. Thinly sliced meat threaded onto skewers was stirred into hot broth, making a swishing sound as it simmered. Centuries later in 1995, a restaurant in Osaka, Japan began serving this "hot pot" to its patrons, and it quickly rose in popularity. They named the dish "Shabu Shabu" which means "swish, swish" in English.

In 2002, long-time ski local Kevin Valaika convinced his brother Bob to relocate from Aspen to Park City. These two restaurant veterans wanted to serve up a new style of dining on Park City's historic Main Street, one that would reflect the very nature of Park City's lifestyle. Kevin's sharp business mind and Bob's culinary expertise influenced by acclaimed chefs like Charlie Trotter and Nobu Matsuhisa, combined to create one of Park City's most distinguished and creative restaurants. Shabu has earned praise as one of the "Top 12 New Restaurants in America" by Conde Nast Traveler in 2005 and "Best Restaurant in Park City" by Salt Lake Magazine in 2006.

Just like freestyle skiing or mountain biking found in a mountain town, Shabu experiments with eclectic menus to showcase "Asian Freestyle" cuisine, a global fusion of fresh ingredients and unique flavors. In addition to their extensive sushi menu, Shabu features popular dishes like Shabu Shabu Hot Pots, Miso Glazed Black Cod, Shabu BBQ Ribs, Coconut Crusted Tofu, Blistered Green Beans and Poke Salad. A gluten-free menu is also available.

Enjoy great food, late night sushi and one of the largest sake selections in the state of Utah in a cozy atmosphere surrounded by a wall-length fierce dragon and metal fish sculptures by local artist Scott Whitaker.

CHEF BOB VALAIKA

Executive Chef Bob Valaika first developed an appetite for Asian cuisine at age 15 when he landed his first job at Benihana of Tokyo. Earning a Culinary Arts degree from Kendall College, he perfected his skills at upscale establishments like Chicago's Café Provencal and Melange, working with notable chefs like David Jarvis, Emeril Lagasse and Nobu Matsuhisa. Valaika moved to Aspen, Colorado and became head chef at Kenechi and Matsuhisa Aspen, receiving formal training from Chef Nobu himself.

In 2002, Bob joined his brother Kevin in Park City and launched Shabu, an award winning restaurant featuring Valaika's own progressive style of Asian cuisine that fuses ingredients from around the globe.

Shabu's "Freestyle" Asian menu is flavored by Park City's mountain lifestyle and the Valaikas' passion for skiing and biking.

Coconut Crusted Tofu

1 block extra-firm tofu
1 cup flour

2 eggs, beaten
2 cups sweet shredded coconut
4 Tbsp olive oil

3 bowls
cookie sheet

Preheat oven to 375 degrees.

Drain tofu and cut into four 2-inch wide slices or "planks." Line up three separate bowls. Place flour in first, 2 beaten eggs in the second, and shredded coconut in the third bowl.

Dredge each tofu slice in flour, then dip in beaten egg mixture, then cover with shredded coconut. Set aside. Heat olive oil in skillet over medium high heat, waiting until oil sizzles with a drop of water. Fry the coconut encrusted tofu slices in olive oil until each side is golden brown. Place on cookie sheet and bake 5 minutes at 375 degrees. Serve with vegetable stir-fry and sweet soy sauce.

Serves 2

WINE PAIRING *PATTON VALLEY VINEYARD, Patton Valley pinot Noir, (Willamette Valley, Oregon) 2014.*
This dry, light Pinot Noir has a bright cherry flavor to start but finishes with darker notes of soy and clove. It is a perfect pair with the liteness of the tofu and the flavors of the sweet soy sauce.

Poke Salad

½ cup lite soy sauce
1 cup unseasoned rice vinegar
2 Tbsp yuzu juice (Japanese tart lemon bitters)
4 Tbsp fresh squeezed lemon juice

¼ cup sweet chili (Mae Ploy brand liquid found at Asian markets)
1 lb Maguro tuna cut in 1-inch cubes
¼ cup seasoned prepared seaweed
1 carrot, julienned

¼ cup sliced green onions
¼ cup sliced English cucumber
¼ red onion, thinly sliced
Tobiko or toasted sesame seeds

Whisk together soy sauce, rice vinegar, yuzu juice, lemon juice and sweet chili (can be made ahead and stored in covered container in refrigerator for up to 2 months).

Combine tuna, seaweed, julienned carrot, green onions, cucumber and sliced red onion in bowl and add soy marinade. Toss and sprinkle with tobiko or toasted sesame seeds.
Serve cold or at room temperature.

Serves 4-6

WINE PAIRING *HAKATSURU Premium Sake, Junmsi Dai Ginjo (Osaka, Japan). Hakatsuru has been brewing sake since 1743. The smooth body and light acid are a perfect complement to the bright flavors of the poke salad.*

POKE *Poke (pronounced po-keh) meaning "cut piece" or "small piece," is a simple raw fish salad that originated with Hawaiian fishermen who cut their catch of raw fish into cubes and then seasoned it with whatever was on hand. It's the classic road food, served as an appetizer or simple meal at grocery stores, surf shacks, restaurants and even gas stations. It started appearing in cookbooks in the early 1970's, and celebrated chef Sam Choy hosts a poke festival and recipe contest every September, receiving inventive variations from as far away as Canada, the mainland, and the South Pacific.*

MAGURO *is the Japanese name for tuna. There are different types ranging from canned to the expensive sushi grade. There are many kinds of tuna in the world, and they all have different tastes.
Use the highest grade when eating raw Maguro tuna.*

Sweet Miso Glazed Black Cod

1-2 lbs cod fillets, 6-7 ounces each (may substitute sable fish)

MISO MARINADE
4 ½ cups sugar
1 cup sake
1 cup Mirin (sweet sake found at liquor store)
5½ cups white miso (Shiro Miso)

Day One

In large saucepan, combine sugar, sake and Mirin over medium heat and whisk until sugar is totally dissolved. Turn heat to medium-low and whisk in White Miso. Stir constantly until mixture is the consistency of a soft paste. Cover and cool completely or overnight in refrigerator.

Day Two

Place fish in glass casserole dish or bowl. Spread marinade over each fillet, liberally coating all sides. Reserve remainder of marinade in separate covered bowl and chill. Marinate coated fish for 48 hours in refrigerator. The sugar in the marinade acts as a cooking agent, essentially "curing" the fish.

Day Four

Preheat oven to 425 degrees. Remove fish from bowl. Rinse in cold water and pat dry with paper towels. Place on foil-lined cookie sheet. Liberally spoon or brush reserved Miso Marinade on each fillet. Bake at 425 degrees for 20 minutes or until golden brown with a caramelized, crispy outer layer.

Tip

Line cookie sheets with aluminum foil to prevent difficult clean-up from caramelized sugar.

Serves 4-6

WINE PAIRING *DUTTON GOLDFIELD WINERY, Dutton Ranch Chardonnay, (Sonoma Valley California) 2014.*
This Chardonnay is gold in color and has the aroma of green apple and lemon zest. The full bodied mouth feel is rich, silky, and elegant. This distinctive weight and creamy texture are a perfect complement to the richness of the miso glazed black cod.

Shabu's BBQ Ribs

smoker
1 rack bone-in pork short ribs (we like to use Kurobuta Pork—the most highly prized pork in Japan—from Snake River Farms)

BRAISING LIQUID
2 Tbsp olive oil
1 onion, diced
5 sticks lemon grass stalks, minced
2 Tbsp fresh ginger, chopped
2 cloves fresh garlic, minced
1 ½ quarts ketchup
1 ½ quarts apple juice

BARBEQUE SAUCE
1 onion, diced
2 Tbsp garlic, minced
1 cup soy sauce
1 cup molasses
1 ½ cups brown sugar
2 Tbsp Dijon mustard
1 cup vinegar
¼ cup chili garlic sauce (Tobanjyan) or Thai Sambal sauce

Shabu's BBQ Ribs are a three part process: Smoke, Sauté and Braise.

Pre-heat oven to 250 degrees.

Smoke

Season pork ribs with salt and pepper. Place in smoker with Applewood chips and smoke at 130 degrees or medium heat for 4 hours. When done, place ribs in roasting pan.

Sauté

In large pan, heat olive oil over medium heat. Sauté diced onion and lemon grass stalks for 2 minutes. Add chopped ginger and garlic. Add ketchup and apple juice and stir to combine.

Braise

Pour braising liquid over ribs in roasting pan so ribs are fully submerged. Bake at 250 degrees for 6 hours.
Remove ribs from roasting pan and place on platter.
Heat olive oil in large pan over medium heat. Sauté diced onion and garlic for 3 minutes. Add braising liquid to pan. Add soy sauce, molasses, brown sugar, mustard, vinegar and chili garlic sauce to pan. Reduce heat to low and simmer, stirring occasionally, until liquid is reduced and thickened to barbecue sauce consistency. Brush BBQ sauce onto ribs. Great served with honey hoisin cornbread and watermelon salad.

Serves 4.

WINE PAIRING *SARACINA WINERY, Atrea Old Soul Red, (Mendocino California) 2013.*
The zinfandel in this red blend gives the wine flavors of black berry, plum, and cracked black pepper. The rich body, color, and taste of the blue/black fruit and light peppery finish pair well with the mild spice of the braising liquid and barbecue sauce.

Blistered Green Beans

MISO MARINADE
4½ cups sugar
1 cup sake
1 cup Mirin (sweet sake found at liquor store)
1 Tbsp chili garlic sauce/ (Sambal) (to taste)
5½ cups white miso (Shiro Miso)

2 Tbsp olive oil
1 lb fresh green beans, trimmed
peanuts, crushed

In a large saucepan, combine sugar, sake and Mirin over medium heat and whisk until sugar is totally dissolved. Turn heat to medium-low and whisk in Chili Garlic sauce (Sambal) and white miso. Stir constantly until mixture is the consistency of a soft paste.

In a large sauté pan, heat olive oil over high heat. Add beans and rotate/stir with tongs until blistering, about 4 minutes. Remove from heat and pat dry. Place in serving bowl and toss with miso marinade. Add more or less marinade according to your taste. Top with crushed peanuts and serve.

WINE PAIRING *HONIG WINERY, Sauvingnon Blanc (Napa Valley, California) 2015.*
The Honig Vineyard and Winery is a family-owned business focused on great wine making, family and sustainability. This sauvingnon blanc has a light body, bright acidity and wonderful fruit flavor. The body and flavor of this wine complement the mild heat and crisp texture of the blistered green beans.

SAMBAL *is a hot sauce made from a mixture of different types of chili peppers with additional ingredientts such as shrimp paste, fish sauce, garlic, ginger, shallot, scallion, palm sugar, lime juice, and rice vinegar or other vinegars.*

SNAKE
CREEK
GRILL
SNAKE
CREEK
GRILL

SNAKE CREEK GRILL

H

Named after a creek that runs nearby, Snake Creek Grill is located at 650 West 100 South, Heber City, in the former Heber Creeper Railway Village now known as Heber Old Town. The turn-of-the-century styled building feels like a friend's living room, with warm, earth-toned colors: sage green wainscoting, gold walls, 30-year old pine and fir wide planked floors and a hodgepodge of antiques and funky collectibles. The restaurant is comprised of three squeaky-floored rooms with an open design. A handsome copper topped bar that seats four or five people is nestled in the entry parlor where you are kindly greeted. This room also features one large table known simply as "the couch," since a comfortable sofa makes for luxurious seating on one side of the dining table. Two other dining rooms offer a nice selection of booths adorned with red velvet pillows, and a selection of tables that seat between two and eight diners. "The Valentine Table" for two is tucked into a corner by the window and features a sultry pink fringed lamp that customers adore. White linen tablecloths and fresh flowers add to the ambience.

Reflecting a down-to-earth style, everything about Snake Creek Grill is relaxed. Service is casual, yet professional. Servers offer sound, no-nonsense advice, yet don't miss providing detailed touches. Owner/Chef Dean Hottle frequents the dining room after dinner is made to offer a personal touch to the cozy dining environment, visiting guests to ensure each are content with their meal and their dining experience.

Dubbed by one local publication as the "Best Park City Restaurant Not in Park City," Snake Creek Grill has fast earned a reputation for offering gourmet food at everyday prices, in a relaxed, casual atmosphere that provides four-star service and cuisine.

CHEF DEAN HOTTLE

Dean M. Hottle is the executive chef and owner of Snake Creek Grill located in Heber City's Old Western Village. His love of food and wine has created one of the most highly respected restaurants in the Wasatch Back. Chef Hottle is a graduate of the Culinary Institute of America at Hyde Park, New York. He came to the Heber Valley in 1999 to work with Chef Barb Hill in the kitchen of Snake Creek Grill. Furthering his culinary career in Utah, Hottle accepted an executive chef position at the Stag Lodge in Deer Valley. In 2007, Hottle's passion for food & wine led him to purchase the award winning restaurant from Hill. Dean brought his culinary vision to Snake Creek Grill with fourteen years of fine dining experience. Chef Hottle prefers to create menus using local and organic ingredients in his restaurant, homes & private events.

Sweet Chili Grilled Kale Salad with Avocado Lime Vinaigrette

5 white golf shrimp per serving (or desired shrimp)
1 Tbsp olive oil
1 Tbsp sweet chili sauce

AVOCADO LIME VINAIGRETTE
1 Tbsp honey
1 garlic clove
1 shallot
½ cup cider vinegar
½ cup cold water
1 large avocado
1 bunch cilantro
1 Tbsp Dijon mustard
¼ cup grapeseed oil (vegetable oil can be substituted)

1 bunch of kale, de-stemmed & chopped
2 Tbsp pumpkin seeds
2 Tbsp crumbled feta cheese
8 halved cherry or pear tomatoes
¼ sliced red onion
3 Tbsp black beans

TORTILLA STRIPS
8 corn tortillas
½ cup olive oil

Preheat oven to 350 degrees. Pre heat grill.

Coat shrimp with olive oil and grill. Toss with sweet chili sauce and let chill in refrigerator. Can be made one day ahead of time. Chop kale and set aside in refrigerator to chill.

Avocado Lime Vinaigrette
In a blender, add honey, garlic, shallot, cider vinegar, water, avocado, cilantro and Dijon mustard and blend for 30 seconds. Slowly add grape seed oil. Transfer from blender to small container. Can be made a few days ahead of time.

Tortilla Strips
Slice corn tortillas into strips. Toss with olive oil and bake at 350 degrees for 5 minutes.

Assembly
Toss kale with desired amount of dressing and top with pumpkin seeds, feta cheese, tomatoes, red onion black beans and grilled shrimp. Garnish with tortilla strips.
Serve in large bowl, or plate individually.

WINE PAIRING *ILLUMINATION Sauvignon Blanc (Napa Valley, California) 2013.*
This Sauvignon Blanc blend is a perfect addition to this salad. A glass of this will have a vibrant nose of citrus and fresh herbs, thus giving way to lush tropical aromas of star fruit and lychee, and the delicious scent of honeysuckle. On the palate, the wine is supple and rich, complemented by bright acidity through the long finish. This should give you a fantastic break of sweetness from the acidity of the dressing, complementing the dressing well.

Roasted Garden Tomato Mug of Soup with Fresh Mozzarella & Aged Balsamic

15 large ripe garden tomatoes, large cubes
1 yellow onion, chopped
3 carrots, chopped
2 stalks of celery, chopped
5 cloves of garlic
1 shallot

2 Tbsp olive oil
3 qts low sodium chicken or vegetable stock (personal preference) low sodium
6 sprigs of fresh thyme, cleaned & chopped
3 sprigs of fresh oregano, cleaned, chopped

2 Tbsp salt
¼ tsp black pepper
¼ cup fresh mozzarella cheese, diced
¼ cup aged balsamic, 10 year or older

Pre Heat oven to 450 Degrees.

In a large bowl toss the chopped tomatoes, onion, carrots, celery, garlic and shallot with olive oil.
On a roasting pan, place vegetables in oven to roast for 15 minutes.
Place roasted vegetables in a large pot with the chicken or vegetable stock. Add thyme, oregano, salt and pepper then simmer for 45 – 60 minutes.
Let soup cool down a few minutes after simmering. Pour soup in a blender and puree. You may need to do this a portion at a time depending on your blender size. After all soup is pureed, return soup to pot and bring back to simmer.

Assembly

Serve in large mugs garnished with fresh mozzarella and aged balsamic vinegar.
This recipe yields enough soup for Snake Creek Grill's evening guests, so feel free to cut ingredients in half.

WINE PAIRING *Renato Ratti Barbera D'Asti (Piedmont, Italy), 2011. This deliciously smooth Barbera will pair perfectly with the soup. A wine with an intense, ruby red color allows for a bouquet of ripe fruit with an undercurrent of spices. This smooth low tannin red from Italy is full flavor with long persistence finish.*

Grilled Buffalo Tenderloin, Maine Lobster Oscar

BÉARNAISE SAUCE
¼ cup champagne vinegar
1 tsp garlic, chopped
1 tsp shallot, chopped
½ lb melted butter
3 egg yolks
1 juiced lemon
1 Tbsp tarragon, chopped
1 tsp salt
dash cayenne pepper

BUFFALO
two 9 oz buffalo tenderloin
¼ cup melted butter
¼ cup soy sauce
2 cloves garlic, chopped
kosher salt & pepper

LOBSTER
2 Tbsp butter
2 Tbsp dry white wine
2 Maine lobster tails

GRILLED ASPARAGUS
6 spears asparagus
½ Tbsp olive oil
kosher salt
black pepper

Béarnaise Sauce

In a sauté pan over medium low heat bring vinegar, garlic and shallots to a simmer for one minute. Continue cooking until shallots are translucent, 1 to 3 minutes longer.

Melt butter and transfer to a liquid measuring cup that has a spout. Separate eggs and combine egg yolks, lemon juice and 1 Tbsp of warm water in a blender. Puree egg mixture for 30 seconds. With blender running very slowly pour in hot butter, continuing to run blender one minute after all the butter has been added. Pour sauce into bowl and stir in vinegar, shallot, garlic mixture. Add in tarragon and season with salt and cayenne pepper.

Tenderloin Soy Marinade

Preheat grill to high heat.

Melt butter. Mix melted butter, soy sauce and garlic then let cool.

Place tenderloins in cooled soy, butter mixture for two minutes.

Remove tenderloins from soy mixture, and season with salt and pepper. Place filets on grill and turn to medium heat. Cook 7 minutes per side for medium rare.

Remove steaks from grill, and let rest 5 minutes before serving.

Grilled Asparagus

Drizzle asparagus with olive oil and season with salt and pepper. Grill asparagus for two minutes.

Lobster

Broil lobster. Pull the lobster meat from the tails, and rough chop lobster meat.

Melt butter, mix with white wine and toss with lobster meat.

Assembly

Place steak on plate, add three asparagus spears on top. Pile lobster on steaks, and top generously with Béarnaise sauce. Garnish with fresh chives.

Serves 2.

WINE PAIRING *CHATEAU ROUGET (Right Bank, Bordeaux, France) 2003. This right bank Merlot blend is a fantastic pairing with a Steak Oscar. As a little older vintage, it allows for the Merlot grapes to mellow out and give way to a delicious aroma of mocha and black cherry. You will also get a bit of smoke and earth. The wine is a perfect balance of fruit and earth, perfect for this dish.*

Pistachio & Chive Crusted Wild Alaskan Halibut

1 cup chopped pistachios
1 cup panko bread crumbs
2 Tbsp diced chives

1 Tbsp salt
¼ tsp black pepper
2 eggs, beaten

1 cup flour
2 Tbsp olive oil
four 6 oz skinless filets of halibut

Preheat oven to 350 degrees.

Combine pistachios, bread crumbs, chives and, salt and pepper together in a shallow baking dish and stir.
Place eggs in one large flat dish and flour in another dish.
Dredge each halibut portion in flour, then eggs, then pistachio bread crumb mixture.

Heat olive oil in a sauté pan over medium heat. Place halibut carefully in hot oil and sear until golden brown, approximately 3 to 4 minutes.
Flip fish gently, then place pan in oven for approximately 7 to 8 minutes.

Serves 4.

WINE PAIRING *PETER MICHAEL L'Après-Midi (Sonoma County, California) 2013.*
This amazing display of California Sauvignon Blanc will really bring out the best in this dish. The wine has a rich flavor of passionfruit, mangosteen, guava, and honeysuckle. There is also a touch of dry honey and candied anise. A rich and zesty wine that gives a long and elegant finish.

Strawberry Rhubarb Pie

PASTRY
2½ cups bread flour, plus additional for rolling dough.
2 Tbsp sugar
½ lb butter
2 tsp salt
1 cup cold whole milk
½ tsp cider vinegar

PASTRY COATING
1 egg
¼ cup cream

FILLING
½ cup butter
1½ lbs rhubarb, trimmed & sliced into ¼ inch pieces
3 pints of strawberries
¼ cup flour
1 cup sugar

Pastry

In a food processor, combine flour, sugar, and salt, and pulse to blend, then add butter and pulse until butter is in pea size chunks.
Remove dough from food processor and place into a large bowl. Add milk and cider vinegar and slowly fold in by hand (if dry add more milk).
Turn pastry dough out onto a floured surface and form into a ball. Wrap pastry dough and refrigerate for 30 minutes to rest.
Roll dough out into a round, flat shape, as thin as possible. Fold dough in half from top to bottom and left to right until you have something that resembles a square. Roll dough out again from square trying to get as close to round again as you can. Spray a baking sheet with nonstick cooking spray and transfer dough to sheet. Let dough rest again in the refrigerator for ten minutes.

Filling

Melt butter in large sauté pan, add rhubarb and half of the sugar. Cook until soft, stirring occasionally for about 6 minutes.
Place strawberries in a large bowl and mix in remaining sugar, flour, and cooked rhubarb.

Assembly

Place strawberry rhubarb mixture in the middle of pie pastry on the baking sheet.
Fold sides up over the top making five sides. Pastry should resemble a star. There should be a small opening at the top to allow steam to escape.
Beat egg, and cream together and brush onto pastry on all sides.
Bake at 425 degrees for 35-40 minutes, rotating baking sheet half way through the cooking process.

Serves 6

WINE PAIRING *Lanson Pink Label: (Champagne, France) N/V.*
This racy pink sparkling wine is perfect with the pie. The nose on this glass is of rose and berry notes. Along with chalky undertones you also get the flavors of crushed raspberry and apricot, fresh ginger, biscotti and ground spice. This wine will give a great balance between the rhubarb and the strawberry.

tupelo

tupelo

TUPELO

MS

With doors opening onto vibrant Main Street, Tupelo lets you sit back, unwind and soak in the fresh flavors of Park City and beyond. When dining here, you're whisked away on a culinary journey without ever leaving the table. Born of one chef's passion for food terroir, Tupelo celebrates globally inspired dishes and locally sourced artisanal produce.

Chef and co-owner Matt Harris creates captivating dishes, blending culinary finesse with a deep appreciation of quality ingredients. After rising to top chef at critically acclaimed restaurants, he traveled across the country and to far-flung locales to find fine food at its source and meet skilled small-batch producers. He tromped through the muddy fields of pig farmers and waded in waters with fisherfolk—all in pursuit of the very best the earth and oceans have to offer.

A true farm-to-table dining experience, eating at Tupelo—whether for lunch, dinner or Sunday brunch—never fails to delight the palate. Each bite tells a vivid story through unexpected flavors and a dedication to delivering mouthwatering food, straight from source to plate.

Full-flavored and thoughtfully prepared, the food served here radiates their makers' identity. From juicy Maine Mussels to luscious Snake River sirloin steak to the punch of Asian-inspired Thai pickled tomato Nam Prik to smoky Italian Pecorino and Porcini mushrooms, each dish explores the ability of food to tell a perpetual story.

In this cookbook, Matt shares the secrets of the most popular dishes on his summer menu. You'll love the flavor burst of Maine crab fritters spiked with hot sauce butter—it thrills with every mouthful. Dinner orders rack up each night for the succulent sous-vide sirloin in our "Beef and Barley" main. And while a plate of compressed watermelon salad could be the most delicious way to cool down on a hot summer's day, honey and spice Madeleines—made by Shirley Butler, Tupelo's endlessly talented pastry chef—wraps up a meal on the sweetest of notes.

CHEF MATTHEW HARRIS

Intuitive and adventurous, Tupelo head chef/co-owner Matt Harris honed his culinary talent while cooking for an impressive panel of uber-chefs: Jean-George Vongerichten, Kevin Rathbun and Pano Karatassos. His passion for sustainably sourced, artisanal cuisine spurred him to open Tupelo in 2015.

Chef Matt's unique dishes capture the rich, colorful stories of his global travels. An advocate of slow food and farm-to-table cuisine, Matt ventures across the country and beyond to meet culinary craftspeople who put pride into what they make—from farmers to fisherfolk, winemakers to cheesemongers.

Matt has appeared on CBS' *Fresh From the Kitchen* as a celebrity guest chef, and in Food and Wine, SKI, Esquire and more.

tupelo

Maine Crab Fritter with Hot Sauce Butter

HOT SAUCE*
35 oz red bell peppers, seeded
7 oz red finger chilies, seeded
2 tsp garlic
2 tsp orange peel
4 tsp salt, divided
8¾ oz Braggs Apple Cider Vinegar
*make at least 12 hours ahead of time

CRAB FRITTER MAYONNAISE
2 egg yolks
1¼ tsp celery seeds, finely ground
2 tsp lemon juice
½ tsp Tabasco® Green Pepper Sauce
1 tsp Tabasco® Original Red Sauce
1 tsp Worcestershire Sauce
1 tsp salt
1½ Coleman's Mustard Powder
7 oz sunflower oil

CRAB FRITTER MIX
2 lbs Maine crab meat
1 crab fritter mayonnaise
5 eggs, beaten
6 cups panko bread crumbs

HOT SAUCE BUTTER
1 part hot sauce from recipe
1 part butter, softened at room temperature

Hot Sauce

Combine bell peppers, chilies, garlic, orange peel and two teaspoons of salt in a food processor and puree until you get a rich, chunky texture.

Pour the mixture into a stainless steel container, seal it up tight and leave it in a warm spot for at least 12 hours. This gives the mixture time to ferment and brings out the delicious flavors.

Once the mixture tastes rich and spicy, stir in the cider vinegar and the leftover salt. Give it a good whisk to make sure all the ingredients are well combined.

Keep the sauce cool in the fridge until you're ready to serve.

Yields approximately ½ quart of hot sauce.

Crab Fritter Mayo

Combine egg yolks, celery seeds, lemon juice, green Tabasco® red Tabasco®, Worchestershire sauce, salt, and Coleman's mustard powder in a food processor, and blend until smooth.

Once blended, slowly add oil and process to emulsify until it is silky smooth.

Crab Fritter Mix

Mix together the crab and all of the crab fritter mayonnaise. Portion mixture into 2 tablespoon size balls.

Beat eggs. Roll crab ball in egg mix, then roll in panko bread crumbs. Reserve in fridge until ready to fry.

Heat fryer to 350 degrees. Add crab fritters, being careful not to overload, and fry until golden brown.

Hot Sauce Butter

Soften butter to room temperature. Combine one part freshly made hot sauce from recipe to one part butter.

Blend until creamy and emulsified.

Assembly

Warm hot sauce butter. Ladle into serving dish. Add four crab fritters per serving. Garnish with pickled peppers or vegetables of your choice (pickled Fresno chiles or okra are Tupelo favorites).

Serves five-4 piece servings

WINE PAIRING *Sean Marron recommends:*
GRUET, Méthode Champenoise Brut Sparkling Wine, (New Mexico).
"This delightful dry sparkling wine that is made in the style of a French Champagne offers a textural contrast to the dish, with the wine's crisp acidity counterbalancing the rich textures of the dish while refreshing the palate for the next bite."

tupelo

Compressed Watermelon Salad, Mint, Basil, and Sorghum Dressing

MS | S

PICKLED WATERMELON RIND & COMPRESSED WATERMELON
1 lrg watermelon
1 lrg Cryovac or FoodSaver bag
1 cup apple cider vinegar
1 cup sorghum syrup (or honey)

SORGHUM DRESSING
¼ cup apple cider vinegar
¼ cup Champagne vinegar
¼ cup sorghum syrup (or honey)
1 pinch salt
1 tsp black pepper
½ cup extra virgin olive oil

GARNISH
1 cup mint leaves, roughly torn
1 cup basil leaves, roughly torn
¼ cup extra virgin olive oil
sea salt and pepper to taste
½ cup feta cheese (we recommend Gold Creek Feta)

Pickled Watermelon Rind & Compressed Watermelon

Separate watermelon fruit from rind.Cut rind into small cubes. Place rind in bag, add vinegar and sorghum, and vacuum on high setting. Set aside and reserve for 24 hours.
Cut watermelon flesh into large cubes (approximately 1½ inches), then place in bag and vacuum it on a high setting.

Sorghum Dressing

In a large mixing bowl, whisk together the apple cider vinegar, Champagne vinegar, sorghum syrup, salt, and pepper. Slowly pour in the olive oil, whisking well to ensure all the ingredients are thoroughly mixed.
Taste the dressing for seasoning and adjust it to your taste.

Assembly

In a large bowl, combine compressed watermelon, pickled watermelon rind, feta, and 1¼ cup sorghum dressing. Mix gently to coat.
Place on plate. Garnish with basil and mint, and season with salt and pepper to taste.
Drizzle with extra virgin olive oil.

WINE PAIRING *Sean Marron recommends:*
BROADBENT, Vinho Verde Rosé, (Portugal).
"Made from a blend of indigenous red grapes - mostly Borraçal- this fruit-driven and slightly spritzy dry rosé has red fruit flavors that offer a natural complement to the flavors of the watermelon, and just enough richness to stand up to the feta cheese without overpowering it."

SWEET SORGHUM *is made from the stalks of the sorghum grass which contain a high sugar content. It is grown primarily for forage, silage, and syrup production and is sometimes called "molasses" or "sorghum molasses," although molasses is actually a byproduct of sugarcane or beet sugar extraction.*

tupelo

Grilled Collard Green Caesar Salad

DRESSING
1 Tbsp water
1 Tbsp Dijon mustard
1 Tbsp grapeseed oil
2 Tbsp extra virgin olive oil (using a mixture of oils keeps the olive oil from being overpowering)
1 Tbsp red wine vinegar
2 anchovy fillets
1 egg yolk
1 Tbsp lemon juice
1 tsp Worcestershire sauce
1 pinch kosher salt

SALAD
8 cups whole romaine lettuce hearts, chopped
4 cups collared greens, whole leaves
1 Tbsp grapeseed oil
1 lemon for zest
chili flakes
smoked parmesan cheese, shaved
rye croutons

Dressing

Blend the water, mustard, oils, vinegar, anchovy, egg yolk, lemon juice, Worcestershire sauce and salt in a blender until you get a light, fragrant dressing.

Salad

Preheat grill.
Wash the collard green leaves well and cover sparingly with grapeseed oil to prepare for grill. Lightly cook on a hot grill, then chop into bite size pieces.
Wash romaine lettuce hearts well and mix with grilled collard greens together in a large bowl.

Assembly

Add dressing to salad mixture and toss to coat.
Add lemon zest to the dressed greens, and sprinkle the chili flakes and Parmesan cheese on top.
Just before serving, garnish with the croutons for an irresistible crunch.

Serves 4

WINE PAIRING Sean Marron recommends:
SCHLOSS GOBELSBURG, Gruner Veltliner, (Kamptal, Austria).
"One of our favorites for this challenging pairing, this classic salad has so many contrasting flavors and textures that requires a special wine like this, fruity yet dry, rich and very crisp, with a touch of white pepper spice, allowing the wine to stand up to this dish while invigorating your palate."

tupelo

Beef and Barley

GARLIC CREAM
1 cup heavy cream
1 cup whole garlic cloves, peeled
1 cup soy sauce
½ whole dried ancho chili, seeded
1 chinois or cheesecloth

BARLEY RISOTTO
1 Tbsp butter
1 medium onion (Vidalia or white), diced
2½ cups carrots, diced
2½ cups celery, diced
¼ lb barley
3 cups chicken stock
salt to taste

BEEF
four 6-8 oz beefsteaks, any good quality cut works great—indulge with your favorite!
2 Tbsp extra virgin olive oil or canola oil

GARNISH
1 cup squash, cut into small batons
2 cups cherry tomatoes, halved
½ cup fresh parsley leaves, chopped

Garlic Cream
Combine heavy cream, garlic cloves, soy sauce and dried ancho chili in an oven proof pan and cover with foil. Bake in the oven at 350 degrees for 1 hour. Blend until smooth, then push through a chinois or cheesecloth. Set aside.

Beefsteak
Fire up your barbecue or preheat your broiler.
Brush both sides of each steak with oil and season liberally with salt and pepper. Place the steaks on the grill and cook until golden brown and slightly charred. Flip each cut halfway through cooking. (Cook steak to desired temperature.).

Barley Risotto
Preheat oven to 400 degrees. While oven heats, melt butter in a large ovenproof pot over medium low heat. Add diced onions, carrots, and celery and sweat until tender and translucent, stirring occasionally to prevent browning. Add barley and continue sweating until barley is translucent, about 5 to 7 minutes.
While barley is cooking, bring chicken stock to a boil in fresh stockpot. Once the barley is ready, remove from heat and pour in the stock. Cover the pot tightly with foil and bake it in the oven for about 45 minutes.
Return the pot back to the stove top and pour in the garlic cream. Simmer over medium heat for about 5 to 10 minutes, stirring non-stop until you get a risotto-like consistency (similar to creamy porridge).

Garnish
Gently heat both cubed squash and halved tomatoes in a pan over medium high heat, retaining a tender crunch.

Assembly
Place a portion of barley risotto into a shallow bowl.
Layer on the steak, and add a spoonful of squash and tomato garnish. Sprinkle with chopped parsley.

Serves 4.

WINE PAIRING *Sean Marron recommends:*
ALLEGRINI, Palazzo della Torre, (Veneto, Italy).
"This fruit-driven rich red wine from the Veneto region in northeastern Italy has enough texture to stand up to the beef while offering plenty of mouth-watering bold dark fruit flavors to keep up with the roasted garlic in the dish."

tupelo

Honey and Spice Madeleines

3 eggs
¼ cup sugar
¼ cup honey, room temperature
¾ cup butter, melted, plus extra for greasing
1 ¼ cup flour, plus extra for flouring
½ tsp baking powder
½ tsp cinnamon
¼ tsp ground allspice
¼ tsp nutmeg, freshly grated
1 pinch Maldon sea salt flakes
powdered sugar
Madeleine tin

Pre-heat oven to 400 degrees.

Grease each Madeleine tin with a dollop of melted butter, sift over some flour, and then pop the tins in the freezer until ready to use.

Madeleines

Crack the eggs into a bowl and pour in the sugar and honey. Beat with an electric whisk on high until the mixture has tripled in volume. For irresistibly light and fluffy Madeleines, keep whisking until you get a pale yellow color.
Gently melt your butter over low heat, then whisk it into the egg mixture.
Fold in the, flour, baking powder, cinnamon, ground allspice, nutmeg, and salt. Make sure the spices are well mixed in.
Retrieve the tins from the freezer and promptly spoon in the Madeleine batter, filling each tin about ¾ full.
Bake in the oven for about 8 to 10 minutes until each sponge is springy to the touch.
Take the pans from the oven and quickly invert them over a wire rack. Delicately tap each Madeleine out of its tin.
Let cakes cool before dusting with powdered sugar and a little salt.

Assembly

Neatly arrange your Madeleines on a decorative plate and serve with a steaming pot of tea.

Makes 24 Madeleines

PASTRY CHEF SHIRLEY BUTLER *Having grown up in the English countryside, fresh ingredients were abundant for Shirley Butler. Year round, she and her family handpicked Brussels sprouts and potatoes, hunted rabbits, caught pheasants, and preserved rhubarb and jams. So for Shirley, the job of head pastry chef at a real farm-to-table restaurant is an essential return to roots.*
As with Tupelo's savory dishes, Shirley's rich desserts emanate from her farflung travels with the distinct influence of native ingredients. They taste like home.
Shirley and her husband Mark moved to Park City in 2000, where she worked as a private chef and then a baker for Deer Valley Resort.
When she's not baking her notoriously fluffy madeleines, Shirley can be found painting large, colorful canvases, playing the flute like a pro, and enjoying the company of her two standard poodles, Melvyn and Wesley.

WINE PAIRING *Sean Marron recommends:*
KIONA, Chenin Blanc Ice Wine, (Red Mountain, Washington State).
"This sweet late-harvest white wine has rich fruit flavors that offer a natural complement to the rich moist texture of the madeleines, while the nuanced citrus fruit flavors of the chenin blanc grape flatter the lemon element of the dish."

WASATCH
BREW PUB
PARK CITY
AMBASSADORS
JULY 4TH CELEBRATION
WASATCH
BREW PUB

WASATCH BREW PUB

WASATCH BREWERY

"Where the hell is the beer? Where are all the breweries?" Those were among the first thoughts Greg Schirf had after hitchhiking to Utah from Milwaukee in the early 80's. Incredibly, drinking and brewing were all but forbidden at the time. So Greg took matters into his own hands and did what any self-respecting Midwesterner would do: he started a brewery. Wasatch was the first craft brewery in Utah – and one of the first in the nation – and has been delighting guests for 30 years and counting.

In 1988, Greg proposed a bill to the Utah Legislature in an effort to reach his thirsty customers directly. With a lot of negotiation and a fair amount of luck, the historic legislation passed and effectively made the brew pub format legal in Utah, forever altering the restaurant landscape. After two years of operating out of their original location on Iron Horse Drive in Park City, Greg was able to open Wasatch Brew Pub at the top of Main Street, where it remains today.

Unlike other brew pubs in the state, Wasatch was built from the ground up to serve as a true pub, providing a blueprint for the many who would follow in his footsteps. Wasatch Brew Pub has been a pioneer in the craft beer revolution ever since its inception. Even in its 30th year, the pub is a Park City mainstay, providing classic fare with a modern and innovative twist, incorporating their own beers into recipes whenever possible.

Expanding into the Salt Lake City market in 2013, Wasatch Brew Pub has again seen major success, drawing new fans with its diverse menu and unrivaled beer selection. Once in desperate need of revitalization, the Sugar House neighborhood has experienced a renaissance in recent years with Wasatch front and center, occupying the iconic corner of Highland and 2100 South.

Though much has changed since the first pints were poured in 1986, Wasatch has remained a constant – committed to quality, ingenuity and pushing the boundaries. "First and Still the Best, We Drink Our Share and Sell the Rest."

CHEF OSCAR BUSTOS

Chef de Cuisine Oscar Bustos moved to Utah in 2000 and has been in the kitchen ever since. Oscar has honed his skills over the past 16 years in various roles in the industry. Prior to joining the Wasatch family, Oscar spent 4 years as Executive Chef at Brio Tuscan Grille. Oscar's expertise has also taken him to other markets around the country, opening stores for California Pizza Kitchen in Las Vegas, Sacramento and New Orleans.

When Chef Oscar isn't flexing his culinary muscle, he's a force to be reckoned with in the boxing ring and on the amateur body-building circuit. Since coming on board with Wasatch in April of 2016, Oscar is enjoying his new Park City community by exploring the local hiking trails whenever possible.

PG172 PG173 PG174 PG175

WASATCH® BREW PUB

Kale & Asiago Dip

½ pound baby kale, stemmed, finely chopped and blanched
8 oz cream cheese, room temperature
3 oz Asiago cheese, shredded
¼ cup buttermilk

2 tsp parsley, chopped
½ Tbsp granulated garlic
1 tsp kosher salt, or to taste
freshly ground black pepper to taste
1 Ciabatta bread loaf

CRUDITÉ (if desired)
celery sticks
carrot sticks
cucumber sticks
bell pepper strips
broccoli
cauliflower
asparagus spears

Pre-heat oven to 350°.

Kale

Chop and blanch kale by quickly placing kale in a pot of boiling water for just a short amount of time and then removing quickly.

Asiago Dip

Mix room temperature cream cheese, shredded Asiago cheese, buttermilk, chopped and blanched kale, chopped parsely, granulated garlic, and salt and pepper in a large bowl until smooth.

Lightly grease a 1 to 1½ qts. baking dish. Spoon mixture into dish and bake at 350 degrees for 25 to 30 minutes or until center is hot, cheese is melted, and the dip has formed a golden brown crust. Let stand 5 minutes. Slice Ciabatta bread into slices and toast.
Serve with toasted Ciabatta slices, crostini or crudité.

Crudité

If you prefer crudité instead of the Ciabatta bread, slice celery, carrots, cucumber, bell pepper, broccoli, cauliflower, asparagus, or vegetables of your choice, and serve with Kale Asiago Dip.

BEER PAIRING *Jalapeño Cream Ale, 4% alcohol by volume. Golden in color, this ale is made with 130 pounds of fresh jalapeños, giving it an intense aroma. The spice of the peppers cut nicely through the fat of the cheese dip, without the burn. This beer is only available on draft at Wasatch Brew Pubs in Park City and Salt Lake City, as well as the West Side Tavern at the Wasatch & Squatters Brewery's in Salt Lake City.*

—Wasatch Brewery

Pub Salad with Honey-Wheat Balsamic Dressing

CANDIED WALNUTS
1 cup whole walnuts
¼ cup confectioners' sugar
1 Tbsp butter

HONEY-WHEAT BALSAMIC DRESSING
½ cup Wasatch Apricot Hefeweizen beer
¾ cup white balsamic vinegar
1 Tbsp Dijon mustard
1 ½ tsp honey
¾ cup canola oil
⅓ cup olive oil
pinch of kosher salt
pinch of freshly ground black pepper

SALAD
mixed baby greens
thinly sliced red onion
red grapes, halved
beehive cheddar cheese, shaved

Candied Walnuts

Put walnuts in a pot and cover with water. Bring just to a boil and remove from heat, strain and place in bowl. Sprinkle confectioners' sugar over the nuts and mix until coated. Melt the butter in a skillet over medium heat, add coated walnuts and cook until golden brown.

Honey-Wheat Balsamic Dressing

Whisk together the Wasatch Apricot Hefeweizen beer, white balsamic vinegar, Dijon mustard, honey, canola oil, olive oil pinch of kosher salt and freshly ground black pepper to taste.

Assembly

On a large plate or bowl, place mixed baby greens, thinly sliced red onion and halved red grapes with candied walnuts and Beehive Cheddar shavings.
Toss with Honey-Wheat Balsamic dressing just before serving.

Other high quality cheddar may be substituted, but we highly recommend this Utah original – the Beehive Cheese Company sits at the mouth of the Weber Canyon and is one of very few remaining artisan cheese makers in Utah.

BEER PAIRING *Wasatch Apricot Hefeweizen, 4% alcohol by volume. "They were dangled before us: big, beautiful, luscious apricots. Our minds said 'No', but our bodies said, 'Yes!'. As usual, we gave in to temptation and created this delicious brew! The subtle fruit sweetness and natural effervescence of Wasatch Apricot Hefeweizen make for the perfect summer salad dressing."* —*Wasatch Brewery*

WASATCH® BREW PUB

Grilled Salmon with Cauliflower Puree and Sautéed Asparagus

four 6 oz salmon filets
1 head of cauliflower, cut into florets
½ cup water
¼ cup half & half
¼ cup heavy cream
2 Tbsp dry vermouth
1 tsp kosher salt
1 lb asparagus
½ lb zucchini
½ lb yellow squash
1 Tbsp extra virgin olive oil
4 oz arugula or as needed
salt and pepper to taste

Cauliflower Puree

In a large pot, combine cauliflower, water, and half & half, and simmer until tender. Strain cauliflower and retain a cup of the cooking liquid for use later. Combine in a blender and puree until smooth, using saved cooking liquid to thin the mixture if needed. Add dry vermouth and mix well. Salt to taste. Keep warm until plating.

Vegetables

Trim the woody stems of the asparagus and cut in 3 inch segments. Slice the zucchini and yellow squash in ¼ inch half-moons.

Begin to sauté vegetables in a pan over medium heat with 1 Tbsp of extra virgin olive oil. Season liberally with salt and black pepper. Add 1 cup arugula, continuing to sauté until the vegetables are tender, but not overcooked, and the arugula is crispy.

Salmon

Lightly coat the salmon with olive oil and season with salt and pepper. Place the salmon filets in a stovetop pan or on a grill and quickly roast. Grill 3 minutes per side for a perfect medium-rare.

Assembly

Start each plate with a generous scoop of cauliflower puree. Top with asparagus, zucchini, and perfectly grilled salmon filet. Top with crispy arugula garnish.

Serves 4.

BEER PAIRING *Ghostrider White IPA, 6% alcohol by volume. "Legend has it the Ghostrider roams Utah's Wasatch Range seeking revenge: someone stole his White IPA recipe. Smooth and crisp, the pale barley and citrusy hops are a perfect complement to this rich salmon dish. It's too good to hide!"*

—Wasatch Brewery

WASATCH BREW PUB

Polygamy Porter Brownie

1 cup all-purpose flour
½ tsp kosher salt
¼ cup unsweetened cocoa powder
3½ oz semi-sweet chocolate
8 Tbsp butter, browned

½ cup Polygamy Porter
4 eggs, at room temperature
1 cup white sugar
1 cup brown sugar, packed
2 tsp vanilla extract

Preheat oven to 350°.

In a large bowl sift together the flour, salt and cocoa powder and set aside.

Meanwhile, melt the chocolate in a bowl over just boiling water. In a small pan over medium heat, melt the butter until it just turns golden brown. Pour the brown butter into the bowl of chocolate, scraping the pan to get the brown bits (this prevents it from overcooking), then add the Polygamy Porter. In a large mixing bowl, beat together the eggs and sugar until thick and shiny, about 2 minutes. Continue beating on low while alternately adding the flour mixture and wet ingredients. Finish with the vanilla. Be careful not to over mix.

Pour the batter into a buttered and floured 9" x 13" pan. Bake at 350 degrees for 40-45 minutes. Top with freshly whipped cream and chocolate sauce, if desired.

BEER PAIRING: *Polygamy Nitro Porter, 6% alcohol by volume. "Meet the sister-wife of our classic brew. This nitrogenated version is as chocolately and as easy drinkin' as the original but even softer and creamier – almost a dessert unto itself."*

—Wasatch Brewery

WOODLAND CASH STORE
WOODLAND
BISCUIT
COMPANY

WOODLAND BISCUIT COMPANY

Set in the peaceful idyllic farming community of Woodland, Utah, the Woodland Biscuit Company is like a tiny oasis of charm and great food. On any given day, you'll find ranchers, campers, bikers, luxury homeowners, tourists and Sunday churchgoers stopping by to socialize and share in the goodness of Laurel Bartmess' homemade buttermilk biscuits. Housed in the historic former Woodland Cash Store, the Woodland Biscuit Company's airy, open interior and flower filled garden patio make it a pleasant destination for a mid-morning drive or bike ride. Laurel's passion for good food is evident in the extra efforts she puts into the menu. She travels out of her way to farmer's markets to find the freshest ingredients instead of buying from large purveyors, even though it costs her time and money. "Quality, local produce is easy to work with. The produce is always beautiful, the taste is superior and the respect I have for farming and farmers runs deep." She is working with local ranchers to supply beef and purchases local eggs and honey from her Woodland neighbors.

The menu is a Southerner's dream! Flakey buttermilk biscuits topped with housemade sweet red pepper jelly and black forest ham (The Hammy), biscuits and chunky sausage gravy, or The Blue, a big biscuit sandwich with a fluffy folded egg, green onions, blue cheese and bacon served with fruit and hash browns or grilled veggies. Or, bring it back to basics with the Sweet Miss Jackie, a big biscuit slathered with butter and homemade blueberry jelly. Even the name conjures up images of magnolia blossoms and plantations. You don't have to be Southern to enjoy this place though; there are other great menu options including Heuveos Rancheros, the Woodland Burger and the Veggie Sandwich plump full of crisp cucumbers, lettuce, tomato, red onion and salt and pepper on toasted multi-grain bread.

The Woodland Biscuit Company—a dream, a destination and an amazing local community!

CHEF/OWNER LAUREL BARTMESS

When asked why she gave up a great, career building opportunity at the University of Utah to open a restaurant in a tiny three-building rural community, Chef/Owner Laurel Bartmess says, "I just have a deep love of food, eating and community that I couldn't seem to shake. The Woodland Cash Store seemed to speak to me from the moment I walked in– 'It needed to be a restaurant.' And, Woodland– well, it's a magical place." As a mother of two daughters, her life would probably have been much easier and safer had she taken the job with the university, but cooking comes from her core, and she believes food is the thread that connects everybody. "I wake up and think, 'What good thing do I get to eat today?'" she says. "And I wanted other people to experience that, too." Her mission is to create delightful food in an atmosphere of sharing and fun social connection. At the Woodland Biscuit Company, she's achieving her dream.

Red Pepper Jelly

2 red bell peppers
1 green bell pepper
¾ cup cider vinegar
1 tsp dried chile flakes
3¼ cups sugar
3 Tbsp powdered pectin

Rinse, core and rough chop red and green bell peppers. In a food processor pulse peppers together until finely chopped (3-5 pulses).

In a heavy bottom pot combine finely chopped peppers, cider vinegar and chile flakes and bring to a simmer for 5 to 7 minutes- enough to soften peppers. Stir in pectin and simmer another 2 minutes while stirring occasionally. Lastly, add sugar and bring to a rolling boil while continuing to stir gently. Keep at rolling boil and stir jelly for 2 minutes. Remove from heat and cool completely in pot before refrigerating.

"Lovely with most everything..... ham, cheddar, turkey, bacon, avocado, fresh, roasted, or grilled veggies, burgers - and of coarse biscuits. Keep refrigerated for up to a month if, it lasts that long."

—Laurel Bartmess

JAM PAIRING *Laurel recommends using her pepper jam on everything and we all agree. Although we would all love her biscuit recipe, there is no need for other recipes from The Woodland Biscuit Company, as the jam makes all her dishes and yours spectacular. Pictured on the feature page are just some of the amazing sandwiches Laurel serves with her Red Pepper Jelly. Create and enjoy. We always do.*

In the warmer months, you will find many cyclists heading out for a beautiful scenic bike ride to Woodland and Kamas. There always seems to be time to refuel at the Woodland Biscuit Company. Now well known as the biscuit ride.

Woodland's best discovery and a must for breakfasts or lunches. Located on Rt 35 in Woodland on the corner of Bench Creek Road and Rt 35.

Restaurant Address and Contact Information

KB **ADOLPH'S** 1
Swiss Alpine
1500 Kearns Blvd, Park City, UT 84060
(435) 649-7177

EP **APEX AT MONTAGE** 11
American Steak House
9100 Marsac Ave, Park City, UT 84060
(435) 604-1300

MW **BLUE BOAR INN** 21
European Fine Dining
1235 Warm Springs Rd, Midway, UT 84049
(435) 654-1400

P **CUISINE UNLIMITED** 31
Catering and special events
2064 Prospector Ave, Park City, UT 84060
(435) 647-0010

CV **DRAFTS SPORTS BAR AND GRILL** 41
Gastropub
3000 Canyons Resort Dr, Park City, UT 84098
(435) 655-2270

CV **EDGE STEAKHOUSE** 49
American Steak House
Westgate Park City Resort & Spa,
3000 Canyons Resort Dr, Park City, UT 84098
(435) 655-2260

MS **FLANAGAN'S** 57
Authentic Irish Fayre
438 Main St, Park City, UT 84060
(435) 649-8600

CV **EPC AT HYATT CENTRIC** 69
Continental
3551 N Escala Ct, Park City, UT 84098
(435) 940-1234

DV **J&G GRILL AT THE ST REGIS** 79
Ranch to Table Steak House
The St. Regis Deer Valley,
2300 Deer Valley Dr E, Park City, UT 84060
(435) 940-5760

KJ **MOLLY BLOOMS** 89
Gastro Pub
1680 W Ute Blvd, Park City, UT 84098
(435) 645-0844

MS **THE MUSTANG** 99
Eclectic American Cuisine
890 Main St, Park City, UT 84060
(435) 658-3975

KJ **MYRTLE ROSE** 109
American Steak House
1456 Newpark Blvd, Park City, UT 84098
(435) 658-0304

CV **POWDER AT WALDORF ASTORIA** 119
American Bistro
Frostwood Dr, Park City, UT 84098
(435) 647-5566

KJ **RED ROCK BREWERY** 129
American Pub/Brewery
1640 Redstone Center Dr, Park City, UT 84098
(435) 575-0295

MS **SHABU** 139
Freestyle Asian
442 Main St, Park City, UT 84060
(435) 645-7253

H **SNAKE CREEK GRILL** 149
Contemporary American
650 W 100 S #6, Heber City, UT 84032
(435) 654-2133

MS **TUPELO** 159
American, Eclectic, Farm to Table
508 Main St, Park City, UT 84060
(435) 615-7700

MS **WASATCH BREW PUB** 169
Brew Pub
250 Main St, Park City, UT 84060
(435) 649-0900

W **WOODLAND BISCUIT COMPANY** 177
Cafe, Breakfast, Lunch
2734 E State Hwy 35, Kamas, UT 84036
(435) 783-4202

CV Canyons Village DV Deer Valley EP Empire Pass H Heber KB Kearns Blvd KJ Kimball Junction MW Midway MS Main Street P Prospector

WASATCH
National
Forest
U.S. DEPARTMENT
OF AGRICULTURE

Book Concept, Design and Production by: Lauren Nadler
Photographer: Pat Cone; Editors: Stephanie Edelman, Corinne Humphrey and Michelle Battaglia

Photography and Illustration Credits: Cover, Main Street store front, Pat Cone; Park City town map, Roger Burrows; pg 3, fondue pot and carrot cake, Shutterstock.com; pg 19, Empire Pass, courtesy of Apex Montage; pg 20, Wasatch Crest trail Biker, Lauren Nadler; pg 29, clouds over Deer Valley and Jordanelle, Bob Christie; pg 30 ,Wasatch Crest Trail Hiker, Lauren Nadler; pg 37, Baramundi watercolor illustration, Gary Gautney; pg 39, walking main street, Pat Cone; pg 40, main street tolley, Lauren Nadler; pg 41-43, Drafts photos, Pat Cone; pg 48, snow scene of Jupiter Peak and Blue Slip Bowl, Pat Cone; pg 57, Flanagan's, Lauren Nadler; pg 58, Guinness, Pat Cone; pg 59, Flanagan's Reuben rolls, ahi tuna, chicken curry, corned beef boxty, Pat Cone; Meatloaf, Shutterstock.com; brownie, Lauren Nadler; pg 66, snow dusting in fall, Pat Cone; pg 67, Skier, Pat Cone; pg 69, Snow scene with aspen and cornice, Pat Cone; pg 69-71, photos, Pat Cone; pg 74, trout watercolor illustration, Gary Gautney; pg 76, mine building, Pat Cone; pg 77, ski tracks and skier, Pat Cone; pg 78 Tubing at Gorgoza Park, Lauren Nadler; pg 87, snow covered trees, Pat Cone; pg 88, horses at Willow Creek Park, Lauren Nadler; pg 89, Piano at Molly Blooms, Lauren Nadler; pg 90, Lamb Chops, Shutterstock.com; pg 91, soup, lamb chops, bread pudding, Shutterstock.com; pg 97, Wasatch Crest hike, Lauren Nadler; pg 98, two horses, Lauren Nadler; pg 107 moose sculpture at Trailside Park, Lauren Nadler; pg 108, Aerialist at Utah Olympic Park, Lauren Nadler; pgs 109-111 Myrtle Rose photos Pat Cone; pg 117, tree snow scene, Phil Archbold; pg 118, Jordanelle Sunrise, Bob Christie; pg 128, Tour of Utah final stage finish, Lauren Nadler; pg 137, sunrise over white barn, Lauren Nadler; pg 138, hikers heading to ski Jupiter Peak, Lauren Nadler; pg 147, biker in Aspens, Lauren Nadler; pg 148, Patrol top of Jupiter Peak, Lauren Nadler; pg 157, tree snow scene, Phil Archbold; pg 158, bee keeper, Lauren Nadler; pg 167, Mt Timpanogas in fall, Lauren Nadler; pg 168, honey jars, Lauren Nadler; pgs 169-171, Wasatch Brewery photos, Pat Cone; pg 176, young skiers and family, Pat Cone; pg 177, Chef Laurel Bartmass, Lauren Nadler; pg 181, Hummingbird, Francis Morgan; Credits page bird soaring, Lauren Nadler; Cover, title page, Snow Background and All Watercolor Illustrations, Shutterstock.com.